FERRARI LEGENDS

Michel Zumbrunn

Text by Richard Heseltine

FERRARI LEGENDS

Classics of Style and Design

MERRELL

LONDON · NEW YORK

First published 2008 by Merrell Publishers Limited

Head office
81 Southwark Street
London SE1 0HX

New York office
740 Broadway, Suite 1202
New York, NY 10003

merrellpublishers.com

British Library Cataloguing-in-Publication Data:
Zumbrunn, Michel
Ferrari legends : classics of style and design
1. Ferrari automobile – History
I. Title II. Heseltine, Richard
629.2'222

ISBN-13: 978-1-8589-4432-6
ISBN-10: 1-8589-4432-5

Produced by Merrell Publishers Limited
Layout by Jade Design
Design concept by Matt Hervey
Copy-edited by Daniel Kirkpatrick
Proof-read by Lucy Bater
Indexed by Vicki Robinson

Printed and bound in China

Jacket, front: Ferrari 860 Monza, see p. 127
Jacket, back: Ferrari F40, see p. 259
Page 2: Ferrari 375 America Ghia, see p. 99
Pages 28–29: Ferrari 860 Monza, as above
Pages 276–77: Ferrari 348, see p. 262

Acknowledgements

I should like to offer my sincere thanks to all the collectors
of Ferrari cars, who, through their collections, are helping
to preserve an important part of Italian culture. I must also
extend particular thanks to Lukas Hüni, Edi Wyss and
Peter Kalikow.

Michel Zumbrunn

I should like to thank Rashed Chowdhury, Bob Hui,
Margaret Heseltine, Giles Chapman, Dave Richards,
Mick Walsh and Mark Ralph for their considerable help
in making this book happen.

Richard Heseltine

Introduction   7

FERRARI LEGENDS   29

The Names Behind the Legends   278

Glossary of Motoring Terms and Styles   283

Directory of Museums and Collections   285

Index   286

INTRODUCTION

With Ferrari, it's all too difficult to distinguish between the actual and the apocryphal. No other marque has garnered a larger, more adoring retinue, one whose devotion borders on religious fervour. Every time the scarlet cars from Maranello win a Grand Prix, the local priest rings the town's church bells to celebrate: Ferrari is enshrined in the national consciousness. And beyond Italy's borders the marque is similarly worshipped with fanatical loyalty, thanks to its unparalleled run of achievements in motor sport over sixty tempestuous years – along with the matchless brilliance, beauty and performance of its road cars. From the every-millisecond-counts firmament of Grand Prix racing to the concours d'élégance automotive catwalks, Ferrari has triumphed.

And how. As the only team to compete in every World Championship Formula One race since the series began in 1950 (some 758 to the end of 2007), Ferrari has accrued more wins (201), drivers' titles (fifteen) and constructors' championships (fifteen) than any of its rivals. Basking in the reflective glow of racing attainment, Ferrari's road-car division similarly continues to overachieve. The current waiting list for a new Ferrari is often two years, and up to four for some hyper-exclusive models; other limited-run editions are sold out before they've even been officially launched.

Yet just having money isn't necessarily a passport to Ferrari ownership. In order to own a new one, you have to get on what is colloquially known as 'The List'. A very limited supply – in 2007 Ferrari built just 6000 cars – and almost unlimited demand complicate matters immeasurably, with some customers paying considerably over the odds to be first on the block with the latest iteration of a Maranello supercar.

It's ironic, therefore, that these egregiously expensive, super-elite machines bear the name of a man whose origins were altogether more proletarian, a man to whom myths and falsehoods continue to cling. But then so it was for most of the lifetime, ninety years of it, of Il Commendatore himself, Enzo Ferrari. Filled with success and adulation, suffering and desolation, his life less ordinary oscillated between triumph and tragedy in equal measure. As Ferrari loyalist, racer, concessionaire and historian

The epic 250GT Berlinetta 'Tour de France' typified Ferrari's coachbuilt offerings in the 1950s, being two parts competition tool, one part toweringly capable road car.

Enzo Ferrari was a competent racing driver, taking several victories at the local level, but never made the leap to superstar status. He soon realized that his real talent lay behind the scenes, forming his own *scuderia* to run Alfa Romeos.

Jacques Swaters once noted: 'He was hard on everybody, including himself. He was a very great man who put everything into his factory and into his cars.'

The man who would in time be deified by the world's car lovers was born into moderate wealth in Modena in February 1898. His father, Alfredo, had eschewed the family business of preparing and supplying delicatessen foods. Instead, he trained as a mechanical fitter and fabricator in Modena railway workshops before setting up his own business. From a small metalwork shop next to the family home, he supplied axles to the Italian railways and earned enough to become one of the first men in Modena to own a car – something that swiftly fired young Enzo's imagination.

As did motor sport. In 1908 Alfredo took his youngest son to a race on the Via Emilia in Bologna, a move that would instil Enzo's lifelong obsession with speed. Unfortunately, in 1916, as Enzo reached adulthood, he would experience the first in a long line of personal tragedies: the death of Papa Ferrari from pneumonia. Later that same year, Enzo's sibling Alfredo Jr passed away in a sanatorium at Sortenna di Sondrio. Emotionally battered, Enzo's mother, Adalgisa, began to dote on her remaining son, and, in future years, it was said that if Enzo took against one of his employees, only Mamma could save their job.

Much as he loved cars, there didn't at first seem much chance of young Enzo making a career out of the nascent automobile industry. He originally dreamed of becoming an opera singer, but this notion was soon thwarted: he just didn't have enough talent. His hopes of making it in journalism fared no better, although, at the age of sixteen, his by-line did appear in *La Gazzetta dello sport*.

And it was at this juncture that Ferrari decided to become a racing driver. After being turned down by the Turin automotive giant Fiat, he eventually took a job at an altogether lower end of the spectrum with a firm that converted Lancia lorries into road cars. His job as a test driver brought him into regular contact with some of the more noted racers of the day. His friendship with former cycling star Ugo Sivocci led to him taking a role alongside Sivocci at the Milan manufacturer Costruzioni Meccaniche Nazionale (CMN), which was involved mainly in reconstructing war surplus vehicles.

It was while at CMN that Ferrari made his competition debut. Although later prone to self-mythologizing, Ferrari claimed he first tasted competition on the 1919 Parma–Poggio di Bercetto hillclimb event, Italy's first motor-sport event after the First World War. It was the country's longest such event, climbing 2723 ft (830 m) in 33 miles (53 km). The twenty-two-year-old steered what was essentially a bare chassis with gusto, ending up eleventh fastest overall. Six weeks later, CMN sent him and Sivocci to Sicily for the Targa Florio road race, where Ferrari endured a torrid time. Legend has it that he was reduced to a fit of rage after being held up by a presidential procession. He was credited with ninth place, but made the finish only after much gesticulating and shouting generally colourful epithets – and waving a gun around. But then this was bandit country. Ferrari's account of the event varied on each telling: the record books state that only eight cars officially finished.

A year later, Ferrari joined Alfa Romeo, the Milan firm with which he would establish previously unthinkable levels of success. Initially Ferrari was a reserve driver only. Repaying his debt to Sivocci, he persuaded his new bosses to add his friend to an already formidable driver line-up. A return attack on the Targa Florio of October 1920 saw him placed second overall in what had proved to be a hellish race. Constant rain in the days leading up to the start had left the road circuit covered in mud and debris. Ferrari drove with brio, recording the fastest lap of the race. Unsure of where he was placed for most of the race, only in the final stages did he become aware that the leader, Guido Meregalli, was twelve minutes ahead. Ferrari then poured his heart and soul into making up the time, clipping four minutes off his rival on the last lap (67 miles/108 km per lap), but he ran out of time. Afterwards Ferrari wept like a baby. If nothing else, the press agreed that with more support – and more accurate timekeeping – he'd likely have won. His star appeared to be in the ascendant.

But it was an event in 1923 that would prove a bridgehead in the Ferrari story. Entered into the Circuit of Savio at Ravenna, Ferrari put on a virtuoso performance, driving out of his skin to win outright and claim the lap record against rivals with much more powerful cars. His efforts were honoured by a fevered crowd that held him aloft. It was on this occasion that the parents of Francesco Baracca – the great First World War fighter pilot – presented Ferrari with their deceased son's Cavallino Rampante (prancing horse) insignia, awarded for his wartime bravery. This badge would go on to become the iconic emblem in Ferrari lore.

Although this account has been debated, Ferrari himself later wrote:

The story of the prancing horse is simple and fascinating. The horse was painted on the side of the fuselage of the fighter plane flown by Francesco Baracca, a heroic Italian pilot who died on Mount Montello: the Italian ace of aces of the First World War. In 1923, when I won the first Savio circuit, which was run in Ravenna, I met Count Enrico Baracca, the pilot's father, and subsequently his mother, Countess Paolina. One day she said to me, 'Ferrari, why don't you put my son's prancing horse on your cars? It would bring you luck.' I still have Baracca's photograph with the dedication by his parents in which they entrusted the emblem to me. The horse was black and has remained so. I added the canary yellow background because it is the colour of Modena.

Whether the story is true or embellished, the distinctive insignia has been applied to all Ferrari road and racing cars. But not before it first appeared on Alfa Romeos. Throughout the rest of the 1920s, Ferrari enjoyed only fleeting success as a driver, often making up the numbers unless he was feeling particularly inspired. More often than not he took part in minor events that he later said made him feel like a trophy-hunter because he often had the most powerful car. He astutely arrived at the conclusion that his true gift was in organizing what went on behind the scenes.

Ferrari's efforts as a driver – but more likely his success as an Alfa Romeo distributor for the Emilia and Marche provinces – had already seen him bestowed with the title Il Commendatore (the term means 'the commended' rather than 'the commander', as is often thought). He was awarded the honour in 1927 by the puppet king Victor Emmanuel III (as a Fascist government honour, it ceased to have meaning after the Second World War), but the tag later took on international resonance as Ferrari entered into legend. Often racing against his customers, most of them being 'gentleman drivers', Ferrari reasoned that it wasn't good for business to finish ahead of them. It was time to settle down, raise a family and not dice with death on mountain roads. He had a flourishing business, and his efforts as a driver had been a priceless preparation for the fabulous career that was to follow.

Il Commendatore maintained Alfa Romeo's relevance as a player in international motor sport throughout the 1930s. His reward was being ousted from his own team, a move that, in turn, laid the foundations for Ferrari – the marque.

SUCCESS BREEDS SUCCESS: SCUDERIA FERRARI IS BORN

Over dinner in a Bologna restaurant, Ferrari, along with Mario Tadini and the brothers Alfredo and Augusto Caniato, set about creating a *scuderia*, a motor-racing team: the brave new world of Scuderia Ferrari was born on 1 December 1929. Although he had by now ostensibly left Alfa Romeo, for at least two more years Ferrari occasionally kept his hand in as a driver, racing under his own name. In 1930 the team entered thirty races and won eight of them.

Thus began a gradual transfer of authority between the manufacturer and its outside competition arm, with Alfa Romeo technicians and equipment leaving for the *scuderia* in Modena. Cash-strapped Alfa Romeo pulled out of single-seater racing altogether in 1933. Its boom-or-boost existence came to a head as control passed to the IRL (Istituto Ricostruzione Industriale), a governmental organization that allowed relative (and that's debatable) operational freedom for the directors of its member firms, which remained state-owned entities. It was left to Ferrari to persuade Alfa Romeo's management to let him continue campaigning with the then-dominant P3 model. Results were immediate, the squad's talisman Tazio Nuvolari winning the Circuit of Alessandria and the Monaco Grand Prix in a season awash with highlights. Add to this an overall win in the Le Mans 24 Hours, and it was a dominant season for the youthful team, with only Maserati and Bugatti providing much in the way of meaningful competition.

Ferrari was by now enjoying wealth and prosperity, but predictably there were bumps in the road ahead. There would be more wins – lots of them – but Scuderia Ferrari faced a new and daunting challenge: the German Nazi Party and its propaganda machine. In a bid to unify the country behind sporting superiority, German firms were bestowed with vast quantities of cash to develop all-conquering racing cars. Against the emergent might of Mercedes-Benz and Auto Union challengers, and their inestimable team budgets, the *scuderia* was suddenly underfunded and outgunned. Despite their efforts – a highlight being Nuvolari's belief-beggaring victory under the noses of Germany's elite at the country's Grand Prix at the Nürburgring in 1935 – the team's drivers usually had to settle for a minor placing when racing at international level.

Matters came to a head in 1937 when, following another changing of the guard at Alfa Romeo, the parent company mounted what passed for a hostile takeover. It bought an 80 per cent stake in the team from existing shareholders. The *scuderia* that bore Ferrari's name was now out of his direct control. Predictably – and understandably – outraged at being usurped, having kept the Alfa Romeo name in the limelight over the course of the decade, Ferrari continued to manage the racing endeavours

Of all Scuderia Ferrari's pre-war victories, few were sweeter – or harder fought over – than that attained by the great Tazio Nuvolari in the 1935 German Grand Prix. His ancient Alfa Romeo P2 beat the might of the local Auto Union and Mercedes-Benz entries under the nose of the Nazi Party.

Manufactured under the alias of Auto Avio Costruzioni, Ferrari's first product was the Tipo 815 sports car. Just two were made, however, as proceedings were interrupted by the Second World War.

amid much rancour with his new bosses. He routinely butted heads with Alfa chief Ugo Gobbato, in part over the hiring of a Spaniard, Wilfredo Ricart, as a technical consultant, but more so over their differences in managerial styles. By 1939 Ferrari's position had become untenable and he walked. Scuderia Ferrari was liquidated.

By now a rich man and full of ambition, Ferrari had bigger fish to fry: he was going to manufacture his own make of car. The only impediment was that, under the terms of his severance agreement, he was barred from building one under the Ferrari name for a further four years. Undeterred, and embittered, he nonetheless pushed on ahead, forming a new company, Auto Avio Costruzioni, that same year. But as storm clouds gathered over Europe, the dream of taking on the world from Maranello suddenly seemed a long way off. Car factories were being handed over for the production of armaments, and shortages of raw materials drastically reduced the Italian automotive industry's capacity for manufacturing civilian vehicles.

As Germany marched on Poland on 1 September 1939 and the stark realities of conflict gripped Europe, all interest in motor racing – in cars in general – dwindled. Alfa Romeo would survive the war years, but as a substantially different company, in time moving further and further away from its roots towards mass production: motor racing was a sporadic distraction only. Enzo Ferrari, however, was only just getting started. His surname was soon to become a byword for motor-sport achievement and the most exotic of all road cars.

FERRARI: BABY STEPS TO MOTOR-SPORT GREATNESS

With the Alfa Romeo payoff burning a hole in his back pocket, Ferrari had forged ahead with his plans for a new car under the Auto Avio Costruzioni banner. Remaining in Modena, he roped in engineer Alberto Massimino to help realize his vision. The former Fiat engineer, who had briefly worked for Scuderia Ferrari during the Alfa Romeo era, was an experienced engine designer and set about creating the new car's 1.5-litre straight-eight engine. With materials being rationed, Ferrari took the pragmatic step of using the Fiat 508C chassis as a basis, with Carrozzeria Touring creating the body from aluminium. The prototype had gone from drawing board to functional reality in just four months, and this haste would hobble the car – and a subsequent sister car – on the 1940 Mille Miglia. Both cars led the 1500-cc class at various points, only to retire. Italy entered the Second World War on 10 June 1940, only a few weeks on from the 1000-mile (1609-km) race, and Ferrari turned his attention to making construction tools and milling machines. Only two of his Tipo 815 sports cars were completed, with hopes for series production coming to naught: Ferrari the automobile manufacturer would have to wait.

Unlike those of many neighbouring states, Italy's motor industry didn't completely disappear during the war, but most of the nation's factories were razed by Allied bombing. Reconstruction was unavoidably protracted, largely because of a shortage of raw materials. Nevertheless, small-series independent marques slowly began to emerge, but these 'etcerinis', as they have latterly been dubbed, lacked vision compared to that of the Ferrari marque.

With a small but talented team behind him, Enzo Ferrari started work on a new – and eponymous – car as soon as Milan was liberated. A new 1.5-litre V12 designed by Gioacchino Colombo was tested in September 1946. *The Autocar* reported: 'News is now at hand of an entirely new make, the Ferrari Type 125. Its specification is in many ways unusual and gives promise of outstanding performance. There will be three models built on a chassis of similar proportions, called Sports, Competition and Grand Prix, respectively.' On 12 March 1947 the initial prototype – minus bodywork – moved under its own power for the first time. In May that year Ferrari scored its first race win in only its second start: Franco Cortese (the Tuscan bearing the unfortunate nickname of 'Chicchino', or 'Country Bumpkin') won the Rome Grand Prix in a cycle-winged 125 Spider.

By early 1948, and following a concentrated period of troubleshooting, the 125 gained an engine displacement hike to 1995 cc (from 1496 cc) and morphed into the 166. This model would establish Ferrari as a legitimate player in international motor sport, winning that year's Targa Florio and Mille Miglia sports-car races. Ferrari also began intermittently making road cars, although he viewed them as little more than a distraction. Such cars were, however, a necessary evil: they helped fund his nascent *scuderia*.

Within a matter of only a few years, what became known as the Ferrari mystique was taking shape. Ferrari's office overlooked the factory gates; that way he could keep an eye on the comings and goings at the fledgling Maranello concern. By 1952 the firm had grown exponentially, with some 250 employees. It was building both race and road cars, and seemingly endless permutations of both. Running a company that bore his own name – being responsible for providing employment for so many people – meant that Ferrari couldn't afford to fail, yet he was still some years away from achieving legendary status.

But the indicators were already there. After Alfa Romeo pulled out of Grand Prix racing, and the regulations were applied to lesser, Formula Two-spec cars, Ferrari cleaned up, with Alberto Ascari claiming the World Drivers' Championship in 1952 and 1953. Being fêted everywhere for his team's success, and patronized by the beautiful people who were queuing up to buy what passed for road cars

After a hesitant start, Ferrari found his feet with the 166 sports and GT cars and their 212 derivatives. The road car market was, however, of secondary importance to the altogether more serious task of going racing.

(most were thinly disguised racing cars), Il Commendatore was already displaying a trait for which he would become notorious: if you wanted to talk to him, it didn't matter if you were a prince or a pauper, you had to come to him. And he would likely treat each visitor in the same manner: make them kick their heels for hours on end and, more often than not, put on a display of haughty arrogance.

Another characteristic that was altogether more fully formed was Ferrari's sense of protectionism. He preferred not to venture out, and left it to others to do his bidding and report back to him. This predictably led to cliques and backstabbing, but no serious damage was ever inflicted on the man or the marque. Tragedy tended to strike closer to home.

Ferrari was forever threatening to throw in the towel, but few ever took his threats seriously. Then, on 30 June 1956, his only (legitimate) son, Alfredo – or Dino – lost his battle against muscular dystrophy and went into renal failure. He was just twenty-four. The entire team went into mourning, and the subsequent line of Ferrari V6 engines became an epitaph, with Dino's signature cast into their cam covers. The fallout for Enzo and his wife, Laura – a noted beauty, who had been born into the landed gentry or made a fortune less respectably, depending on whom you believe – was understandably devastating. Doubly so for Mrs Ferrari, who shortly thereafter was installed in a huge villa that she had to share with her mother-in-law, with whom she constantly quarrelled. Ferrari found respite from the misery in the arms of his long-time mistress, Lina Lardi, who had given him a child in 1945. This child, Piero Lardi, would be publicly acknowledged as Ferrari's offspring only after Laura's death in January 1978.

By the time of Dino's demise, Ferrari the company was under serious pressure, the empire often threatening to crumble to dust as the coffers ran dry. Yet Ferrari, an 'agitator of men and ideas', as he was once described, found a way of moving on – even if not always in the right direction. Ferrari was rarely seen trackside, but he remained very much the embodiment of the team. The *scuderia* in turn reflected its figurehead, and boomed and slumped with disorientating frequency. Drivers came and went (those who didn't die on the track during what was a gladiatorial age), as did designers and team managers. Some more than once.

Yet Ferrari always seemed to land on his feet. After financial pressure caused the Lancia family to sell its marque in 1955, the intervention of several parties (including Fiat) effectively gifted the Lancia's Formula One car and equipment to Ferrari – along with a sizable dowry – with the Vittorio Jano-conceived Lancia D50 bolstering the hitherto rival's fortunes. Ferrari was nonetheless sniffy about what he viewed as a cuckoo in the nest – this despite Juan Manuel Fangio claiming the 1956 World Drivers' Championship title.

The biggest problem facing the *scuderia* by the end of the decade was Ferrari's intransigence. Although willing to fund endless engine-building programmes, using a sort of pseudo-Darwinist approach to weeding out those unfit to serve, he was blindsided by an unwillingness to learn from, and exploit, advances made elsewhere. Often ahead of the game during the early to mid-1950s, by the end of the decade the *scuderia* had been left behind by English upstarts. Ferrari refused to be convinced of the benefits of disc brakes and was resolutely opposed to following the lead of the Surbiton *garagistes* (as he dismissed designers and engineers of humble origin) at Cooper and build a mid/rear-engined Formula One car. There was no way he was going to put 'the horse behind the cart', the net result being that Cooper and driver Jack Brabham walked to the championship titles in 1959 and 1960. Even then Ferrari continued to deride the 'assemblers' from the United Kingdom and their funny little 'kit cars'. At least with the likes of Alfa Romeo or Maserati he was on the same page: in 1951 he had gone so far as to write a letter to his old bosses at Alfa Romeo – the same ones who had disposed of him all those years earlier – expressing his sadness that the company was pulling out of racing. Faced with the onslaught of bright young things from Britain, the Old Man, as he had become known (and not always with affection), was clearly a man out of his own time. But he wasn't about to be put out to pasture. Unblinking Ferrari worship was about to begin in earnest.

UNSTEADY AS SHE GROWS: THE EMERGENCE OF FERRARI ROAD CARS

For most of the 1950s, Ferrari's road-car production consisted of small-series runs, the production of which often didn't reach into double figures. The Maranello firm was a boutique, one patronized by royalty, playboys, movie stars and your common or garden beautiful people. If you wanted a one-off, then no problem: Ferrari typically sold cars as rolling chassis to be clothed by an outside coachbuilder.

In the firm's embryonic years, this coachbuilder tended to be Alfredo Vignale's eponymous concern. Born in Turin in 1913, and apprenticed as a panel-beater when just eleven years old, Vignale worked for Carrozzeria Farina during the 1930s before going it alone at the end of the Second World War. A talented designer in his own right, he often worked closely with prolific freelance stylist Giovanni Michelotti. And while the likes of Ghia, Bertone and others bodied early Ferraris, more often than not it was cars styled by Michelotti and crafted by Vignale that found greater favour.

This symbiotic relationship would, however, last only a few years. While seemingly indifferent to his road-going wares, Ferrari was astute enough to realize that having them completed with an endless array of body styles resulted in a degree of uncertainty over how they would turn out. He wanted a

Battista 'Pinin' Farina and Enzo Ferrari developed an inseparable working relationship during the early 1950s, leading to today's sole authorship by Pininfarina of all production-Ferrari styling.

partner, a *carrozzeria* (body designer and builder) of choice. And it was Vignale's former employer, Battista 'Pinin' Farina, who would assume the mantle of favourite couturier.

As shrewd in business as he was artistically gifted, 'Pinin' had left his brother Giovanni's Stablimenti Industriali Farina concern in 1930 and set up shop in Turin under his own name, as Carrozzeria Pinin Farina (later Pininfarina). By the early 1950s, as the Italian economy entered a boom period, Farina's usually delectable outlines had found a ready and affluent clientele. Farina and Ferrari had known each other since the 1920s, and Farina had long since recognized Ferrari's dominance among sports-car manufacturers. It was natural that the two would join forces. The problem was that neither party wanted to be seen to make the first move, and go to visit the other. After a certain amount of pride was swallowed, they met each other halfway, in Tortona, and hammered out a deal over lunch. After a hesitant start, Farina bodied a trio of 212 Inters in 1952 (one for movie director Roberto Rossellini), followed by a batch of 342s, 375 Americas and 250 Europas, along with several competition chassis cars. It marked the birth of an enduring relationship that continues to flourish to this day.

The alliance gathered serious momentum in the latter half of the decade. While Ferrari's one-off flights of fantasy attracted plenty of positive ink in the motoring monthlies, it was the firm's volume (all things being relative) projects, such as the 250MM (see p. 52), with nominally uniform outlines, that brought in consistent revenue.

And it was in June 1958 that Ferrari and Pinin Farina conspired to create the first truly mass-produced car to wear the Cavallino Rampante: the 250GT. The model's importance in Ferrari lore cannot be overestimated, as it represented a significant move forward for both parties. For the manufacturer, it showed a willingness to build a volume product without deviating from the script and getting distracted by the tailoring of each car to suit a customer's whim. For Farina, the original call for two hundred cars represented stability, a contract that brought with it a guarantee of steady work and a regular source of income. Such were the plaudits bestowed on this new car – John Bolster wrote in *Autosport*: 'I would describe this Ferrari as a superb luxury car, combining great performance with extreme refinement to an almost unapproachable degree' – that the original sales forecasts proved woefully pessimistic. It wouldn't be the first time that demand for a 'catalogue model' would exceed supply.

THE 1960S: ALL HAIL THE KING, BUT PRIDE COMES BEFORE A FALL

Before the 1960s truly started swinging, Ferrari was in turmoil. Its road cars continued to soak up the dictionary's supply of superlatives within the world's motoring media, but the race team was floundering.

Having finally relented and let his designers construct a mid-engine Formula One challenger, the *scuderia* came up trumps in 1961 with the 'Sharknose' 156, with the American ace Phil Hill taking the drivers' title. However, the red cars' dominance that year flattered to deceive.

The change of regulations to a new 1.5-litre formula played into Ferrari's hands, as the team had been using just such an engine since 1957. British rivals were left scrambling to find suitable powerplants and were usually down on power. In addition, most wound up being sidetracked by the large-capacity Intercontinental series – which Ferrari refused to support – that briefly threatened to split Grand Prix racing into two factions. Ultimately, the series folded and there was a return to normality, in this instance a pitched battle in Maranello.

In a year that had witnessed triumph – dominance in Formula One, yet another win at the Le Mans 24 Hours, booming sales of road cars – and tragedy – the death of the *scuderia*'s popular German ace, Wolfgang 'Taffy' von Trips – nobody expected what was coming. In November 1961 Ferrari let it be known that eight of his senior directors were now seeking alternative employment. These included his chief engineer, Carlo Chiti; experimental design department chief, Giotto Bizzarrini; sales manager, Girolamo Gardini; and racing team manager, Romolo Tavoni. The news spread like wildfire, and it proved to be just the first in a series of seismic shocks that would threaten to unseat Ferrari.

The man who unintentionally kicked off the whole furore was Gardini. A modest and unfailingly polite man, this Ferrari loyalist had worked for Enzo since the Auto Avio Costruzioni era and had become his sales manager in 1950. Considering his success in the role, and the length of his relationship with the boss, it's no great surprise that he was a respected – and well-liked – man at the Maranello works, one with plenty of allies.

The 342 America was typical of the small-series road cars produced by Ferrari during the 1950s, built to satisfy the whims and fancies of the elite. In the 1960s the firm moved towards product unification, and the bespoke tailoring gradually became a thing of the past.

Gardini's adversary – and for most of those involved in the saga, the root cause of the 'palace coup' – was Enzo's wife. In 1959 Laura Ferrari became a major shareholder in the firm and started to wield her authority, and her special influence. On the one hand she was devoted to her husband, despite all his philandering; on the other she exasperated him and his aides, not least on the occasion when her luggage was left in a Berlin taxi and the team had to stay behind and track it down. Of greater consequence was her attendance at races. As Ferrari's reluctance to leave his hometown intensified, he increasingly relied on accounts from others, including Laura. Bit by bit her meddling began to unsettle the workforce, her erratic behaviour leading to endless arguments with exasperated race bosses and sales staff. The flashpoint occurred when she very publicly slapped the mild-mannered Gardini while venting her anger. Incensed, he demanded an apology. When one didn't prove forthcoming, he marched to the restaurant where Ferrari was eating and laid out an ultimatum: if you don't get your wife under control, I'm walking. Ferrari's response was along the lines of 'goodbye', only not so polite.

At a stroke, the Old Man had heated up a cauldron of trouble. Such was Gardini's popularity (and Laura's unpopularity) that Chiti, Bizzarrini and other managers decided to join together as a united front, and once again an ultimatum was presented to Il Commendatore. Ferrari's response was predictable: he fired them all. These were senior – and talented – personnel, and without them it looked as though the race team in particular would suffer.

Expecting a contrite Ferrari to beg them to return once he'd cooled down, the 'renegades' were to be disappointed. There was to be some consolation for them, if only of the temporary variety. Within a few weeks of the revolt, a new marque existed: ATS (Automobili Turismo e Sport), with Gardini, Chiti and (briefly) Bizzarrini among its number. With their background in both Formula One and the road-going sports-car market, great things were expected. Unfortunately, expectation and actuality were mutually exclusive. Having poached drivers Phil Hill and Giancarlo Baghetti from Ferrari to lead the attack on the 1963 World Championship, the team suffered a singularly dismal maiden season. Lead driver Hill finished only one race, and the team failed to score a solitary championship point. Its 2500GT road car, however, electrified everyone who witnessed its Geneva Salon unveiling that same year.

The first ever mid-engined Italian road car – and one of very few offered anywhere in this configuration – this brave V12 machine could exceed 150 mph (241 km/h), and those members of the press lucky enough to test one raved about the experience. Griff Borgeson enthused in *Road & Track*: 'Thanks to the absolute perfection of the car's performance in every way, I have never felt safer in a car at high speed, nor have I been more impressed.' Unfortunately, ATS's financiers had massively overstretched themselves, and this, combined with a clash of egos among the principal players, saw the firm turn turtle in 1964.

Predictably, Ferrari was unmoved. Road-car production was booming as the firm fully embraced the concept of mass production, even if the annual figures tended to be akin to the hourly production of a major Detroit player. Trackside, the *scuderia* had bounced back from potential calamity, with former motorcycle racing superstar John Surtees claiming the 1964 Formula One World Drivers' Championship (thanks in no small part to the engineering genius of the youthful Mauro Forghieri). Italy's economic miracle was in full swing and Ferrari prospered: the marque was king of the hill on the track and in the luxury GT road-car market. Enzo Ferrari had reason to be cheerful. But storm clouds were gathering. Once again he was about to set in motion a series of events that could topple his precious *scuderia*. Simultaneously, outside forces were to have a potentially catastrophic effect on the market for extravagant automobiles.

BUTTING HEADS WITH THE BLUE OVAL, AND AN END TO PROSPERITY

It seems improbable now, but in 1963 Ford almost became the majority shareholder of Ferrari. And it was Enzo who made the initial approach, albeit by the very Cold War thriller-esque method of sending a representative to doorstep the German consul in Milan. Word eventually reached Detroit and Ford's general manager, Lee Iacocca, who had already laid the groundwork for Ford's Total Performance programme: the marque of the Blue Oval would triumph in everything, everywhere, and bask in the reflective glow. 'Win on Sunday, sell on Monday' became the mantra. By taking over Ferrari, or at least the bulk of it, the Ford Motor Company could bypass the start-up process. In addition, there were endless opportunities for cross-species tie-ins and limited editions. On the other side of the fence, the Old Man would have the protection of a major manufacturer and enough finance for his ever-expanding competition programme.

It didn't quite work out that way. Marathon negotiations between the sixty-something Italian autocrat and the fourteen-man, small-print-minded delegation of Detroit execs ended in disarray. Notoriously ambivalent in his attitude to the United States, Ferrari buckled at the eleventh hour, proclaiming: 'My rights, my integrity, my very being as a car manufacturer, as an entrepreneur, as the leader of the Ferrari works team, simply cannot work under the enormous machine, the suffocating bureaucracy of the Ford Motor Company.' Reaction from the Italian media – from Italians in general – served only to cement his place as a national hero. Ferrari – the marque – was a precious jewel and needed protection from the gunslingers and bean-counters from Detroit.

Enzo Ferrari's failure to accede to the Ford Motor Company in the boardroom led to the Detroit giant implementing its Total Performance programme. The resulting GT40 annihilated the Italian cars in the French endurance classic, variations of the model winning every year between 1966 and 1969.

Not that Henry Ford II or Iacocca was going to take being jilted at the altar without looking for some payback. Within a week of being snubbed, Iacocca had created a taskforce and a feasibility study: just how much would it cost to give Ferrari a drubbing at Le Mans? A great deal as it happens, but the automotive giant's coin attracted a cadre of super-talented men, and all with the intention of besting the red cars in the 24-hour classic, a race that had been a Ferrari benefit for the first half of the decade (Ferrari won every year from 1960 to 1965). Indeed, it was a constant source of dismay to the Ferrari lead driver John Surtees that such emphasis was placed on this one race; Grand Prix wins tended to occur after June. Le Mans mattered to Ferrari – a lot.

Charged with designing Ford's new challenger was former architect Eric Broadley. Within ten years, this British talent had gone from winning the 750 Motor Club's 1172-cc championship with a homebuilt special to entering Formula One under the Lola banner. His beautiful mid-engined sports-prototype, dubbed simply the GT, provided the kernel for what became the GT40. Powered by a small-block Ford V8 engine, it didn't altogether cover itself in glory, but it was enough of a calling card to attract Ford: Broadley effectively took a year's sabbatical to create the Anglo-American supercar.

From new premises in Slough, England, Ford Advanced Vehicles – under the watchful eye of former Aston Martin team-manager John Wyer and ex-pat Englishman Roy Lunn, who headed up Ford's Advanced Vehicle Concepts division – entered three cars in the Le Mans 24 Hours in 1964. One retired after a fire caused by a ruptured fuel line, the other two with gearbox issues. As control of the project passed to the sainted American former racer Carroll Shelby on the West Coast, and the Lunn-fronted Kar Kraft in Michigan, a revised and substantially more powerful version arrived in time for the following year's running. Six cars were entered, and all failed to finish.

Then it happened. In 1966 Ford finished 1-2-3. Variations of the GT40 theme went on to win every year to 1969; Ferrari hasn't won at Le Mans since. The might and colossal spending power of Ford had humbled Ferrari. Ford was about to inflict an even bigger blow, commissioning British engine-builder Cosworth to produce a Formula One engine that would be available to any team. Debuting in 1967, the DFV (Double Four-Valve) V8 unit would go on to power 155 Grand Prix winners to 1983. For such a company as Ferrari – one that built its own chassis, engines, transmissions, everything – the economies of scale soon proved untenable. Enzo Ferrari realized he needed a partner, a firm with financial clout that could protect the company from a whole raft of social problems that had begun to blight Italian industry – not to mention the threat from a new challenger from just up the road.

MORE TRIALS LIE AHEAD AS FIAT RIDES TO THE RESCUE

Just as Enzo Ferrari was dismissive of ATS, he was indifferent to the latest pretender to his kingdom: Lamborghini. Legend has it that Ferruccio Lamborghini became a motor manufacturer only because he was outraged at being kept waiting for hours on end by Il Commendatore when paying him a visit. A self-starter, and endlessly inventive, he had made his money manufacturing tractors and air-conditioning units, and enjoyed the fruits of his labour, buying more than one Ferrari – all of which proved unreliable. After being rebuked by Enzo, Lamborghini decided to go it alone and teach him a lesson. The truth is probably more prosaic: there was more glory having your name attached to a 150-mph-plus (241-km/h-plus) sports car than on a mud-plugging farm implement.

In much the same way as the Maranello marque had been slow to react to the arrival of British pre-eminence in Formula One, Ferrari was seemingly oblivious to what many outsiders saw as a changing of the guard. When Lamborghini showed a bare chassis for what became the Miura supercar (the term being coined especially for this remarkable device) at the 1965 Turin Salon, complete with a V12 engine in the middle – and mounted sideways – Ferrari viewed it as little more than smoke and mirrors. It wouldn't catch on. When the finished article was unveiled at the Geneva Salon in March 1966, it seemingly rendered Ferrari products obsolete. It was light years more advanced. It didn't matter that the car didn't work as well as it should; it represented the future. Ferrari responded two years later with the

Ferrari faced another threat in the mid-1960s. Lamborghini, from over the hill in Sant' Agata, unleashed the Miura, which instantly rendered Ferrari's road car obsolete. At least that was the impression lent by the media.

glorious 365GTB/4 (see p. 224), but, with its front-engined layout, this car was widely perceived as being anachronistic. And before long Ferrari would face a whole new onslaught of supercar wannabes. A war was in the offing.

By the end of the 1960s, the market for high-end exotica was at an all-time high, but the sense of euphoria among manufacturers and designers couldn't last. The onslaught of new U.S. safety legislation taxed even major manufacturers, so such a minnow as Ferrari was hit especially hard. Factor in the rise of union disputes – a number of sit-ins, strikes and violent confrontations – and the future didn't appear bright. As rival Maserati sought solace under the protective cloak of Citroën, Ferrari followed its lead and contacted Fiat's boss (and Ferrari customer), Gianni Agnelli. An agreement had been in place since 1965 for Fiat to share the use of Ferrari's Dino V6 engine, and there were plans for further collaboration. Fiat needed an image boost, and Enzo Ferrari, reluctant though he was, knew he needed the money. In 1969 Fiat succeeded where Ford had failed and bought a 40 per cent stake in the exalted marque for $11 million. Enzo retained 49 per cent; Piero Lardi was given 10 per cent, and Sergio Pininfarina 1 per cent. While Fiat would operate the road-car side of the business, Il Commendatore retained control of his treasured race team. By the end of the decade, Fiat's stake had increased to a whopping 90 per cent, but even for those who viewed the move as a predatory one on the Turin giant's part, it guaranteed the marque's future. The financial backing was crucial: the next two decades witnessed a roller-coaster ride of calamity and accomplishment, often concurrently.

TRIUMVIRATE OVER ADVERSITY: THREE KINGS REVIVE FORMULA ONE FORTUNES

As the 1970s dawned, Ferrari hadn't tasted world championship glory since 1964. By the end of the decade, it was once again the dominant force, with only a few fallow years. No team could stay consistently on top, but few could match the force of Scuderia Ferrari during this glorious period. Much of this renaissance was down to three men.

As was typical of Ferrari and its Machiavellian intrigues, Mauro Forghieri had fallen out of favour by the end of the 1960s and was bundled off to special projects. Without him, the Grand Prix squad was left behind, the final straw coming in 1973 when lead driver Jackie Ickx left mid-season, disgusted with his car's lack of performance. Il Commendatore had been ill for the previous twelve months and, predictably, he listened to the Chinese whispers and tittle-tattle. The difference in this instance was that he realized the error of his ways and reinstated Forghieri, who then built the car that would dominate Formula One for the middle part of the decade.

The net result was a Ferrari walkover in 1974 for the other key constituents in the Ferrari turnabout – the Austrian driver Niki Lauda and the team manager, Luca di Montezemolo. Lauda bagged nine pole positions and two wins from fifteen races before claiming the 1975 (with support from Clay Regazzoni) and 1977 drivers' championships (he would likely have claimed the 1976 crown but for a horrific accident at the Nürburgring that led to him being given the last rites).

Montezemolo, meanwhile, had no background in motor racing, but this brilliant young lawyer bought strict order to the chaos, becoming Agnelli's right-hand man and proving his masterful knack for diplomacy by not appearing to subvert the Old Man. He brought hard-headed, in-the-field

The brilliant – and brave – Niki Lauda added lustre to Ferrari's tarnished *scuderia* during the 1970s, claiming two drivers' titles for the hitherto ailing team. Predictably, it couldn't last, and Ferrari's Grand Prix performance declined during the following decade.

The Testarossa and its 512TR derivative proved that supercars could be user-friendly, and both models became automotive pin-ups to all car-obsessed schoolboys during the 1980s. However, this period also saw foreign rivals move ever closer to achieving technological hegemony.

understanding to proceedings, and, once Ferrari got its act together, its rivals didn't see which way the red cars went. Add in the drivers' and manufacturers' titles in 1979 (with Jody Scheckter, ably backed up by the brilliant Gilles Villeneuve) and pride was reinstated to the tarnished squad, one that had long since grown to be Italy's unofficial race team.

The road-car division, however, was busy going through a transitional period. Those small-scale manufacturers that remained in business were being pressed on all sides, whether by the unions at home or by having to reconfigure their wares to meet still uncertain overseas regulations. Just to heap on the

misery, a new local tax was levied on high-displacement vehicles that made them even less attractive to those wealthy Italians still brave enough to be seen driving exotic cars. Then, to cap it all, Ferrari and its rivals took their biggest hit in October 1973: a fuel crisis. Every nation was affected, and the demand for thirsty, high-performance vehicles disappeared overnight. In countries dependent on imported oil, Italy included, everyone felt the consequences. It was going to get worse before it got better.

THE 1980S AND BEYOND: FARCE AND FERVOUR

By the early 1980s the violence and chaos surrounding Italian industry had receded, as union power ebbed. Ferrari had a range of capable machines, the 308GTB (see p. 254) in particular proving a huge hit after its launch in 1975. The arrival of the Testarossa in 1984 was met with a clamour of excitement, as were such limited runs as the 288GTO. Yet while the road-car market recovered – boomed, even – the race team entered one of its customary slumps.

After claiming both 1979 titles, Scuderia Ferrari claimed just eight points the following year. Aside from the 1983 constructors' crown, the 1980s would prove a barren decade: British teams McLaren and Williams built cars that were more advanced, faster and (tellingly) more reliable. The group that had heaped glory on the team in the 1970s had long since disbanded, and there may as well have been a revolving door at the Ferrari technical department, considering the changes in personnel. Factor in the usual political intrigues along with constant pillorying from the Italian media, and a dip became a depression became a trough.

Then, in the early hours of 14 August 1988, Enzo Ferrari passed away in his sleep. He was ninety years old. Remarkable though his achievements were – and that is undeniable – what followed his death was close to disarray. Instead of acknowledging his achievements and realigning the team's focus, parent Fiat used it is a testing ground for managers. With no firm hand at the helm, self-protective timidity became the norm. The hiring of the British design genius John Barnard briefly stopped the rot, and the 1990 Formula One season witnessed six wins, with Alain Prost coming close to claiming the drivers' title. But this was to prove a false dawn. By the end of the following year's campaign, the team had imploded, with Prost, Barnard and two team managers lost in the battle.

SURVIVAL OF THE FITTEST: FERRARI RETURNS FROM THE BRINK

Successful as Ferrari's road-car division had been for most of the 1980s, its products still lacked the technical edge of its German rivals. A global recession in the early 1990s once again saw demand for such

The 'Old Man' died in 1988, his instrumental role in the history of the automobile – and in motor sport – beyond question. His near-legendary status attracts cult-like levels of worship in Italy and abroad, while the cars that bear his name have become synonyms for beauty and performance.

During the 1990s Ferrari began its renaissance, the 456GT being the first model to embrace new methodology and technological advancement with conviction. That it was dizzyingly beautiful only aided its cause.

profligate machines dwindle, but Ferrari weathered the storm. In parallel with the race team, Ferrari was about to undergo an image makeover: a golden period beckoned.

Key to this was Luca di Montezemolo – the second coming. Returning to the fold in 1991, he set about rebuilding a tattered race team, hiring Peugeot's competition head, Jean Todt, and, in turn, the best driver of his generation, Michael Schumacher. The German – by then with only two Formula One drivers' titles behind him – arrived in 1996, bringing with him his trusted technical lieutenants from the Benetton team, Ross Brawn and Rory Byrne. The rest of the decade was a steep learning curve, but, bit by bit, the team became less reactionary and more proactive; distrust of innovation gave way to around-the-clock probing for anything that could lend an advantage. Ferrari had found its ambition again. After claiming the constructors' title in 1999, the team would crush the opposition in the years to come, with Schumacher being crowned World Drivers' Champion every year from 2000 to 2004. Ferrari's approach to winning has become increasingly ruthless, and some would claim that the 'sport' element of motor sport has been conspicuously absent since its return to form, but nobody can argue with the results.

The same goes for the road-car division. Instead of relying on building fast and beautiful cars while paying only lip service to technological advancement and reliability (the cars would still sell, such is the lure of the name), Ferrari has latterly been busy pushing envelopes and breaking moulds. The modern Ferrari road car is a technological tour de force, such models as the F430 or 599GTB Fiorano being imbued with belief-beggaring levels of performance but without the temperamental nature of yore. Ferrari is actively leading the way, each new strain uprooting goalposts and running away with them.

In the new millennium, the awe-inspiring 205-mph (330-km/h) 599GTB Fiorano is a technical marvel, as adept at crossing continents in a single bound as it is at slaying purpose-built racers on track days.

As of 2008, parent company Fiat is on the up-and-up after years of dodging coffins. The prospect of a Ferrari sale – or flotation – seems to have been averted. The Turin industrial colossus currently owns 85 per cent of Ferrari, Piero Lardi 5 per cent and the Mubadala Development Company (a state-owned company of the Abu Dhabi government) the remainder, with the brand being pushed in all manner of new directions. Merchandizing and commercial tie-ins with other firms account for 25 per cent of annual turnover, with everything from teddy bears to perfume and mobile phones to scooters wearing the Cavallino Rampante, complete with a correspondingly high price tag.

And the future? After sixty years of both over- and underachievement, who knows? What is certain is that every new Ferrari, be it road or racing car, has a huge reputation to live up to, not to establish.

FERRARI LEGENDS

1947 FERRARI 166 SPIDER CORSA

After being effectively dethroned from his role as Alfa Romeo's competition tsar in 1939, Enzo Ferrari was barred from building a car under his own name for four years under the terms of his severance. Aside from the Auto Avio Tipo 815, of which just two were made, the future motor mogul would have to wait until the end of the Second World War to realize his car-building aspirations. The car pictured here is widely touted as being the earliest surviving competition Ferrari, the 166 Spider Corsa.

Design and development were by fellow Alfa Romeo old boy, Gioacchino Colombo, Il Commendatore commissioning him to conceive a 1.5-litre V12 engine. The 166 tag refers to the cubic centimetres – or cc – of each of the cylinders; the cc consequently became a classification hallmark of the marque. Work commenced in 1945, but it would be a further two years before the first prototypes were ready, this being the third car made. Fitted with closed-wheel bodywork, the car was driven by Franco Cortese on the Circuit of Modena in September 1947 (the model having debuted at the Piacenza circuit four months earlier), where Cortese set the fastest lap before retiring. A month later, it reappeared with new *cigaro*-style coachwork and an enlarged 1.9-litre Tipo 159 engine, to be driven by Raymond Sommer in the Turin Grand Prix. The French star scored a commanding win at Turin's Valentino Park street circuit, the first victory of international standing for the fledgling *scuderia*.

The car was subsequently reworked during the winter months and sold off in January 1948 as 002-C to Gabriele Besana, Ferrari's first private customer. Engaging the experienced Cortese as a co-driver, Besana entered the car in the 1949 Mille Miglia, but failed to finish. This historic race car currently resides in a Swiss collection.

From small acorns ... Stark, pared back and with only token concessions to civility, the Spider Corsa marked Ferrari's first hesitant steps towards motor-sport greatness.

Opposite: The classic, longitudinally mounted V12 engine was of all-alloy construction and, in period, produced around 130 bhp at 7000 rpm.

Right: The vast steering wheel fronts a plain aluminium dashboard. A sparse array of instrumentation is dominated by the large rev counter, which reads up to 8000 rpm.

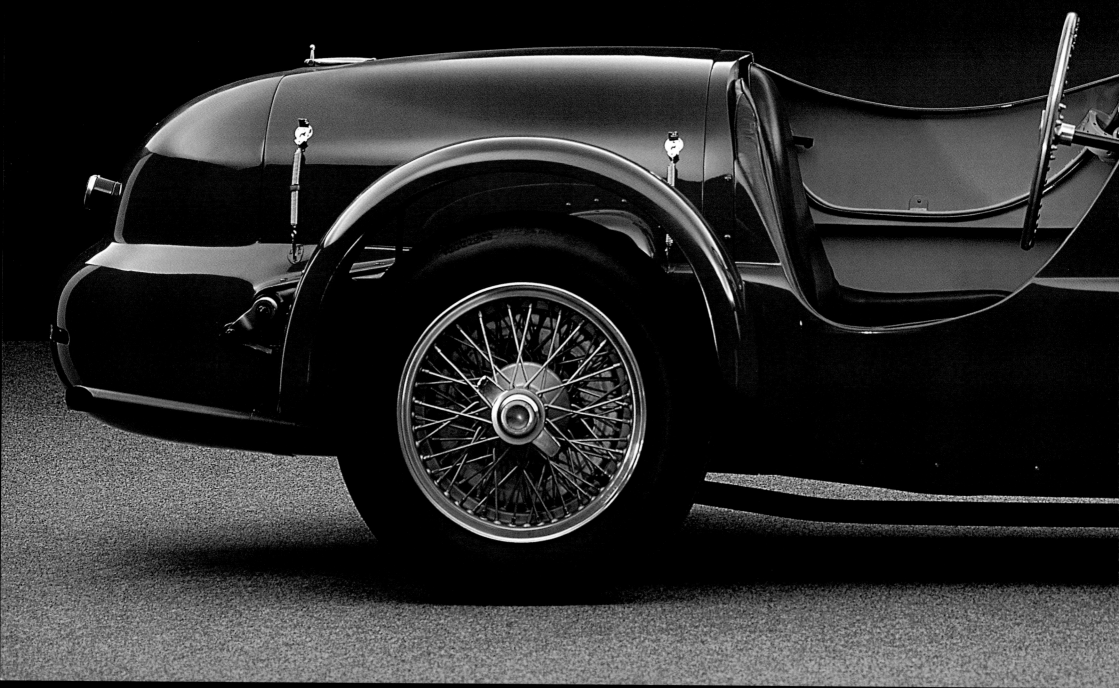

In no way is the Spider Corsa pretty, the rudimentary bodywork being a case of form following function. This example is believed to be the oldest surviving Ferrari.

1951   FERRARI 212 EXPORT

During his firm's emergent years, Enzo Ferrari displayed little interest in building road cars in volume. There was clearly a market for them, but he deemed them a means to an end, a method of raising revenue for his nascent race team. The Maranello firm tended to build small runs for such favoured customers as Count Umberto Marzotto, one of the famous Marzotto brothers who brought great prestige to Ferrari with major race wins during the early 1950s.

Derived from the earlier 212 Inter, the Export featured the same Gioacchino Colombo-designed V12 engine, housed in a tubular-steel frame, but with a much shorter wheelbase. This example was built to Marzotto's brief in March 1951 and featured coachwork by Alfredo Vignale's *carrozzeria* to a design by Giovanni Michelotti. Resplendent in two-tone green, it was among the prettiest of the breed. The car was stripped of anything that could interrupt the flow, even such items as external door handles or windscreen wipers (the shallow, curved air deflector being too small to house any). Similarly, there was no weather protection to speak of, despite the luxurious – all things being relative – cockpit trimmed in tan leather with matching carpeting. In no way was this a stark race car.

Predictably, however, Marzotto couldn't resist giving the car a little exercise, entering it in the July 1951 Dolomite Gold Cup and finishing eleventh on the road and eighth in class. A year later, he returned to finish seventh overall, also winning the Trieste–Opicina hillclimb a few months later. The car's real significance in Ferrari lore, however, is that it was the first example of the marque ever to be evaluated by an English-language publication. In June 1951 a smitten Gordon Wilkins gushed in *The Autocar*: 'It brings tumbling forth the superlatives which a cautious tester tries to keep in reserve for the really special occasions.'

Alfredo Vignale was once the couturier of choice for customers wanting a bespoke Ferrari, this car having been styled by his regular collaborator, the prolific Giovanni Michelotti.

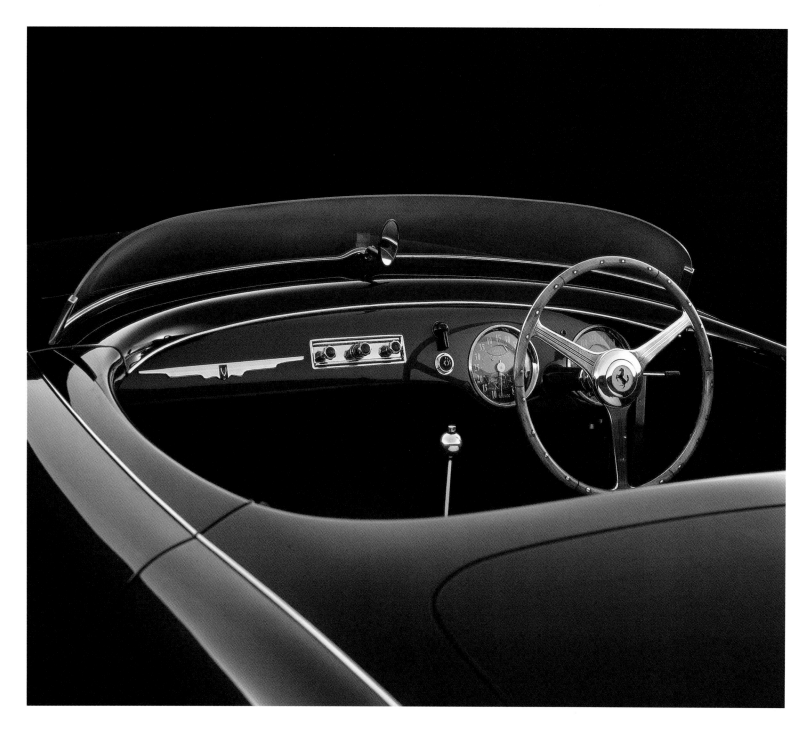

Left: Built primarily for road use, this one-off Ferrari was relatively luxurious for its day, with leather upholstery and carpeting. There was no weather protection, however – not even windscreen wipers.

Opposite: Tiny, gem-like rear lights and delicate chrome detailing are typical of the artistry expected of coachbuilt Ferraris.

With minimal overhangs and few decorative adornments to get in the way, this Vignale/Michelotti co-production is among the prettiest of all Ferraris, itself something of an achievement.

Two-tone green paintwork rather than
the usual Italian Racing Red was highly
unusual for any Ferrari of the early
1950s. This was the first of the 212s to
be road-tested by an English-language
publication.

1952   FERRARI 342 AMERICA

It wasn't a huge success, but the 342 America has a particular importance in Ferrari history, as it represented the marque's first true road car as opposed to a thinly disguised racer. It was produced from late 1952 to the spring of 1953, and never had an official public launch; just six cars were made. The car shown here is of singular worth as it was built for Ferrari's first royal customer, King Leopold III of Belgium.

The 342 America was powered by a V12 engine conceived by Aurelio Lampredi and mounted in a typically rugged ladderframe chassis. The only genuinely unusual feature of this short-run model was that it had the widest track of any Ferrari yet built – 52 3/16 in. (1326 mm) front and 51 7/8 in. (1318 mm) rear – which allowed for a long wheelbase and a more commodious cabin. Alfredo Vignale's Turin *carrozzeria* bodied the first example, with Pinin Farina clothing the remainder. This project marked the beginning of the end of Vignale's official involvement with the marque, and helped establish a Ferrari bond with Pinin Farina that remains resolute to this day. Constructed of steel, aside from the aluminium bonnet and boot lid, the 342 America was produced in both coupé and cabriolet versions, but neither was especially elegant, largely because the radiator was mounted so far forward.

Distinct from its siblings, this particular example – the first to be clothed by Pinin Farina – featured a larger displacement 4.5-litre engine (compared to 4.1 litres for the others), which, according to the factory's claims, produced 250 bhp at 5000 rpm. Leopold was heavily involved during the planning stages and requested several unusual features: the dashboard houses an altimeter in the glove-compartment door and an eight-day chronometer, used by the king, respectively, to measure his elevation while driving over the Alps and to gauge distances travelled as he toured Europe. Leopold retained the car for two years before exchanging it for a 375. More recently it has been restored, and was the winner of the top prize at the prestigious 2002 Ville d'Este Concours d'Élégance.

The 342 America is one of the rarest of all production Ferraris; only six were ever made. This example was created at the behest of King Leopold III of Belgium.

Opposite: Front overhangs and multiple – but necessary – bonnet scoops ensured that the 342 wasn't the most attractive of early Ferraris.

Left: According to Ferrari's own figures, the Aurelio Lampredi-conceived, competition-inspired V12 boasted a displacement of 4.5 litres and produced a heady 250 bhp at 5000 rpm.

Opposite: The opulent cabin befitted perfectly a car built for royalty. King Leopold III himself collected the car from the Maranello factory on completion and drove it back home to Belgium. The instrument sited in the door of the glove compartment is an altimeter.

Below: The 342's styling works best from the rear. Ferrari offered the model in both convertible and coupé configurations, this example featuring fold-down rear seats. The bodywork, save for the aluminium bonnet and boot lid, was constructed of steel.

1953 FERRARI 250MM

It was an act of breathtaking derring-do, and it earned him national celebrity status. Fortified by vast quantities of brandy, and chain-smoking his way over the entire 1000-mile (1609-km) distance, amateur driver Giovanni Bracco won the 1952 Mille Miglia aboard the prototype Ferrari 250MM. In doing so, the wealthy industrialist vanquished the might of the factory Mercedes-Benz team. To honour this achievement, Ferrari produced thirty-two replicas of the winning car, naming the new model Mille Miglia (or MM). This also marked the firm's earliest successful attempt at building cars in anything resembling volume. The MM also spawned the most successful line of GT racing cars to emanate from Maranello: the 250-series Tour de France, SWB and GTO.

Aurelio Lampredi designed the 2963-cc V12 engine, which was fed by three Weber carburettors. The MM had a tubular-steel chassis with an unequal-length wishbone front suspension and a live rear axle. The open Spider configuration had unlovely coachwork by Vignale. But it was the altogether prettier Pinin Farina Berlinetta coupé that captivated: its long bonnet and sweeping fastback silhouette established the template for all Maranello GTs.

This particular example was clothed by Pinin Farina in April 1953, but differed from its sister cars in having a slightly longer nose, a design feature influenced by the then-current 500 single-seater. Predictably – naturally – finished in Italian Racing Red, it was sold new to Luigi Giuliano from Rome for 3.5 million lire. Unlike most of its siblings, however, this car led a sheltered life: its future owners included a film production company that used it for chauffeuring film stars around Italy. Having been used only sparingly for its intended motor-sport function (hillclimbs, mostly), it has never been crashed, modified or restored. This places it in rarefied company for a competition Ferrari.

This fabulous creation differed from other 250MMs, having a longer nose that aped Ferrari's then-current Grand Prix cars.

250 *millemiglia*

Opposite: The car's outer beauty was mirrored internally by the Aurelio Lampredi-designed V12. Fed by three Weber carburettors, it produced around 240 bhp in period.

Below: Pinin Farina's artisans created a beautifully proportioned outline with an expansive glasshouse and no extraneous styling tinsel.

Left: The large fuel cap was in place for competition use, although this example led an altogether more sheltered life and was campaigned only sporadically.

Opposite: Despite its predictably stark cabin, this car was once used to chauffeur movie stars around Italy. If not altogether luxurious, this Ferrari didn't lack for glamour.

The beautiful MM marked the genesis of the 250-series line of Ferraris, and was built to honour the marque's success on the Mille Miglia road race.

1953   FERRARI 250 EUROPA

Though road cars were still viewed as a means to an end, an expedient process of raising funds for his racing endeavours, Enzo Ferrari realized that some degree of uniformity was necessary if the marque was to move forward. Building one-offs and small-series runs was profitable but ultimately time-consuming and often overly complex. Although the Europa was in no way a volume product, it incorporated an infinitely more cohesive methodology than the preceding 166 and 212 models in terms of bodywork and interiors. Closely related to the 375 America (see p. 90), both cars being unveiled at the October 1953 Paris Salon, it shared the same tubular-steel ladderframe chassis with a 110 3/16-in. (2799-mm) wheelbase. Both models were the largest Ferraris to date, the Europa using a 3-litre Lampredi V12. Performance was electrifying for the period, the factory claiming a top speed of 135 mph (217 km/h) and 0–60 mph (0–96.5 km/h) in a little over eight seconds.

After twenty cars had been completed, Ferrari ushered in the second-series edition in time for the 1954 Paris Salon. With a noticeably shorter 94½-in. (2400-mm) wheelbase, and a switch to the less bulky Colombo V12, the result was still patently a road car – few Europas were ever raced, although one finished third in the 1956 Tour de France – but an appreciably more agile one. Some twenty-four of these cars were made, with just one example in right-hand-drive configuration.

Significantly, the Europa marked a sea change in the relationship between Ferrari and Alfredo Vignale's *carrozzeria*. Once the favoured couturier to the Maranello firm, here he was usurped by Pinin Farina. Vignale would clothe just four first-generation cars, and a single second-series edition. The remainder – including a lone convertible – were the work of its Turin rival.

Markedly less racer-inspired than other contemporary Ferraris, the Europa represented for the Maranello firm a step towards series production rather than small batches and one-offs.

Elegant, and with a high beltline and low roofline, Pinin Farina's take on the Europa set the template for future GTs bearing the Prancing Horse badge. The Turin styling house subsequently became Ferrari's favoured coachbuilder, a bond that remains unbroken to this day.

The body-coloured fascia and Nardi wood-rim steering wheel are typical of any 1950s Ferrari; the supplementary gauges mounted in the centre of the dashboard are unique to this particular car. Note the shallowness of the side glazing.

1953 FERRARI 375MM PININ FARINA SPIDER

Essentially a series of models, all sharing the same numerical designation and all conceived by Aurelio Lampredi with a V12 powerhouse derived from Grand Prix cars, the 375-series resulted in some of the most spectacular Ferrari race and road cars yet witnessed. The nomenclature correlated to its 375 cc per cylinder displacement, MM predictably relating to the Mille Miglia road race that was fast becoming a Ferrari monopoly. The first example was fielded by the factory in the 1953 Senigallia sports-car encounter, where Luigi 'Gigi' Villoresi lapped some fourteen seconds faster than the outgoing 340MM. And, while the initial prototype was bodied by Alfredo Vignale's *carrozzeria*, subsequent production cars – or what passed as such – were bodied by Pinin Farina in either open or coupé configurations.

Unlike the 340MM, the new strain was a much more stable car at speed and consequently proved popular with privateer drivers (owner-drivers not associated with a factory team) – at least those who could handle 340 bhp. One such was Masten Gregory, who owned this car in the 1950s. Having been entered by the works squad in the Buenos Aires 1000 km season opener in 1954, where Giuseppe Farina and Umberto Maglioli came out on top, it was then sold to Gregory, the 'Kansas City Flash', who shipped it Stateside. The bespectacled – and abnormally brave – driver then crashed it in practice for a race at Pebble Beach, Florida. The car was returned to the factory for repairs before Gregory embarked on a sporadically successful campaign in Europe and the United States. It subsequently found more success in the hands of its ensuing owner, Gregory's brother-in-law, Dale Duncan. The car continued to be competitive at the local level into the early 1960s, and more recently it has been seen trackside at historic racing events.

Rugged, super-quick and blessed with bestial beauty, this particular Pinin Farina Spider was bought from the factory team by bespectacled American racer Masten Gregory – also known as the 'Kansas City Flash' – who had it painted in his customary white-with-black racing stripes.

Below: The Pinin Farina outline borrowed heavily from previous competition Ferraris, the cutaway sides and shallow doors typical of most sports-racers of the period.

Opposite: The cabin, seen here with a metal tonneau cover over the passenger compartment, was typically basic and most likely cramped for the lanky Gregory.

Left: Masten Gregory drove this car to four overall race wins during the 1954 season in Europe and the Bahamas.

Opposite: Unlike some of its siblings, this 375MM didn't feature a headrest fairing. Alfredo Vignale clothed the first example, while subsequent editions were the work of Pinin Farina.

1954 FERRARI 375MM 'ROSSELLINI'

In the 1950s it was not untypical for a racing car to be reworked and reclothed in a bid to remain competitive. In this instance, the rebodying exercise was aimed at civilizing a sports-racer for road use. That it was built for the legendary film director Roberto Rossellini, and was the first non-competition car commissioned from the coachbuilder Sergio Scaglietti, only adds to its importance in marque lore. This car was unlike any other 375MM.

Rossellini bought the car in the spring of 1954 after the factory had finished using it as a development hack. Originally a Pinin Farina-bodied Spider, and painted bright red, the fearsome 4.5-litre V12 racer came to a sticky end only a few months later after it connected with a palm tree and suffered front-end damage. On its return to the Maranello works, the chassis was straightened and the front suspension repaired before the bare frame and running gear were dispatched to Scaglietti's Modena *carrozzeria*, which was then barely a year into what would become an enduring relationship with Ferrari.

Taking the better part of twelve months to complete the work, Scaglietti crafted a dramatic coupé outline from aluminium, the greenhouse and rear deck following the style of the contemporary Mercedes-Benz 300SL. The creases behind the front wheelwells anticipated those of the 250 Testa Rossa (see p. 142), and the large vents in the flanks served to dissipate heat build-up from under the bonnet.

The rebodying exercise was completed in January 1956, and Rossellini would retain the car until July 1964 (this reputedly being his favourite of the seven Ferraris he owned, starting with his first in 1949). Its next keeper, Mario Savona from Sicily, had it repainted green, although in the 1990s – and two owners later – it was returned to its original grey splendour.

This dramatic, one-off coupé was crafted by Scaglietti for movie auteur Roberto Rossellini. It began life as a racer and was re-clothed after the Italian drove it into a tree.

Below: The maroon leather contrasts beautifully with the grey, body-coloured interior metalwork. Instruments are typically sparse, with switches for such items as windscreen wipers and foglights sited beneath the dashboard.

Below, right: The mammoth race-bred V12 produces around 330 bhp at 6500 rpm, the ugly air cleaner partially obscuring three Weber carburettors, the height of which necessitated the bonnet scoop (opposite).

1954 FERRARI 750 MONZA

Always a canny operator, Enzo Ferrari was fully aware that there was money to be made from producing racing cars for the privateer driver: in this particular instance, variations on the theme would prove highly lucrative. In 1953 he authorized the construction of two prototypes bearing the less-than-romantic nomenclature 'Tipo 375', with engines derived from the 2.5-litre four-cylinder 625 Grand Prix car engine. These development mules proved quick, if not altogether reliable, during sporadic race outings, but, at the end of the year, the decision was made to adopt the closely related 555 Supersqualo unit instead. Enter the 750 Monza, so named after its 750 cc per cylinder displacement and the location of its debut victory in 1954.

With only a brief front-line career as a works entry, which included a win over a strong Lancia team in the 1954 Tourist Trophy (for Mike Hawthorn/Maurice Trintignant), the 750 Monza more than lived up to its role as a customer racing car. Future activities were in the hands of privateers, and in this fashion the car amassed an impressive run of successes, at both the national and the international level, up to the end of the decade, with some thirty-two cars made in 1954–55.

One such owner-driver was American Masten Gregory, who owned this example. The car was finished in the U.S. racing colours of white and blue; the Kansas ace scored several wins and podium spots with it during the mid-1950s, including finishing third in the Bari Grand Prix behind two Maseratis, second in the Portuguese Grand Prix at Oporto and first overall in the Lisbon Grand Prix in 1955. The next owner, Loyal Katskee of Omaha, had the car painted black and continued racing it until 1959, with several wins in U.S. races.

Scaglietti clothed the fearsome Monza; this example was raced in period by American Masten Gregory.

The Monza is beautiful in profile, sharing styling cues with the 500 Mondial and 860. Originally finished in red, Gregory added white stripes before having it resprayed in a white-and-blue livery that denotes American racing colours.

Following an extensive rebuild, and the reinstatement of Gregory's white-with-a-blue-teardrop paintwork, this survivor from the gladiatorial era of sports-car racing has been actively campaigned in recent years in historic motor-sport events.

1954 FERRARI 500 MONDIAL

Closely related to the 750 Monza (see p. 79), and nearly identical visually, this esteemed sports-racer was nonetheless significantly different beneath the skin. Aimed largely at privateer drivers, it borrowed heavily from the super-successful Tipo 500 single-seater, not least in its 1985-cc (later also 2.5-litre) four-cylinder engine conceived by Aurelio Lampredi. To distinguish the new model from its Formula Two/Grand Prix car inspiration, it was christened 'Mondial' – or 'World' – in honour of the two world championships accrued for the *scuderia* by the great Alberto Ascari in 1952 and 1953.

The prototype featured an outline sketched out by Alfredo 'Dino' Ferrari (although this has been debated) and interpreted in aluminium by Carrozzeria Scaglietti, but Pinin Farina was initially chosen to body production Mondials with a silhouette based on the bigger V12 sports-racers. Production would ultimately revert to Scaglietti, but using the Pinin Farina design.

Extremely light at just 1590 lb (721 kg), and agile, the Mondial made its race debut in the Casablanca 12 Hours in December 1953, Ascari and Luigi Villoresi coming home second behind a considerably more powerful Ferrari 375MM. Perhaps the model's greatest result was the runner-up spot for Vittorio Marzotto in the following year's Mille Miglia (won by Ascari in a Lancia D24). In a bid to remain competitive, for 1954 the Series II edition was initiated, with revisions that included larger carburettors, coil-sprung front suspension instead of the previous leaf-sprung set-up and a new five-speed transaxle.

This example was one of two Mondials originally owned by Porfirio Rubirosa, a sometime diplomat for the Dominican Republic, now remembered largely for his many dalliances (his final marriage was in 1965 to the then nineteen-year-old actress Odile Rodin; he was 56). He raced this, his second Mondial, in the 1954 Carrera Panamericana road race with American Ernie McAfee, but failed to finish. The following year, he entered the Sebring 12 Hours but crashed out after fourteen laps. His competition career ended shortly thereafter.

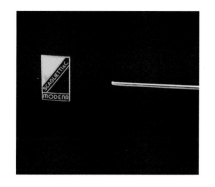

Designed with owner/entrant racing drivers in mind, the delicious Mondial was bodied by Scaglietti to a design by Turin's Pinin Farina.

Opposite: Although built for competition use, the Mondial was among the prettiest cars of the 1950s, the aluminium coachwork being ultra-thin to save weight. The outline was in period attributed to Alfredo 'Dino' Ferrari, but this has since been disputed.

Right: The Mondial's jewel-like four-cylinder engine was designed by the then-omnipresent Aurelio Lampredi, and was closely related to those found in contemporary Ferrari Grand Prix cars.

This car was raced in period by playboy Porfirio Rubirosa, a notorious womanizer who had dalliances with, among others, Marilyn Monroe, Ava Gardner and Kim Novak. Rubirosa wasn't a great racing driver, and died at the wheel of a Ferrari near his Paris home in 1965.

1955 FERRARI 375 AMERICA 'AGNELLI'

Despite Enzo Ferrari's notorious ambivalence about the United States, he quickly realized that North America was awash with the moneyed and a likely buoyant market for his cars. The 375, with its large-displacement V12, was a natural fit, and, on breaking cover at the 1953 Paris Salon, the America edition was appropriately bold, given its intended marketplace. Closely related to the 250 Europa, which was launched concurrently, in time the model would sport a variety of body styles – none more unusual than this remarkable device created by Pinin Farina for a local playboy: Gianni Agnelli.

Cultured, athletic and inconceivably wealthy, this scion of one of Italy's great dynasties bought his first Ferrari in 1950, but this was an altogether more unusual machine. Just fourteen Americas were made, and this example was delivered as a rolling chassis to the Turin *carrozzeria* in November 1954. Under the guidance of Franco Martinengo, Pinin Farina's artisans set about creating the eccentric outline. The front-end treatment was particularly unusual and, with its perpendicular grille and elevated bonnet line, unlike any previous Ferrari. Equally distinctive were the wrap-around windscreen and A-pillars that leaned forwards rather than backwards, as was the usual Pinin Farina tradition. The roof featured a glass panel that allowed copious amounts of natural light into the plush, red leather-trimmed cabin; the rear buttresses merged awkwardly into the sloping rear deck. Finished in a dark-green hue, with a deep ruby red for the top of the car, this remarkable collision of styles emerged at the 1955 Turin Salon and was soon scorching the autostrada with its excited owner at the wheel.

Not that he would keep the car for long. In 1959 it was dispatched to Ferrari's North American concessionaire, Luigi Chinetti. It has recently been restored to its original 'out there' wonder.

With its bluff frontal treatment and often clumsy detailing, the 'Agnelli' one-off was no beauty. It remains, however, one of the most easily recognizable of all the 375 Americas.

Opposite: The fabulous, competition-inspired V12 was hugely powerful for its day. From a displacement of 4522 cc, and according to the manufacturer's own figures, it produces a thumping 300 bhp at 6250 rpm.

Below: Unusual buttresses meld uneasily into the rear deck. Fiat heir Gianni Agnelli gave Pinin Farina free rein when designing the car, and its artisans chose to experiment in this manner. Such buttresses were later watered down and used on such production cars as the Dino.

The dark British Racing Green and ruby-red colour scheme was as distinctive as the outline. The wrap-around windscreen was a nod to American cars of the day.

Below, left and right: Being a one-off, the 'Agnelli' is brimful of novel detailing, including the rear window that could be partially cranked down for extra ventilation, and the glass roof panel providing the cabin with extra natural light.

Opposite: The opulent – if only by Ferrari standards – cockpit featured maroon leather and a handsome alloy-spoked Nardi wheel. This Ferrari, although not Agnelli's first, is inextricably linked to the industrialist, and he kept it until the late 1950s.

1955 FERRARI 375 AMERICA GHIA

Representing the final Ferrari to be bodied by Ghia, this remarkable machine more than lived up to the old American maxim of 'it ain't done 'till it's overdone'. Built at the behest of Bob Wilke, a Wisconsin paper products and greeting card mogul, this was more than just a show car; Wilke routinely drove this flamboyant 4.5-litre V12 device as its makers intended. It was also a regular fixture in race-track paddocks, with Wilke sponsoring the winning car in the Indianapolis 500 in 1959 and 1962.

When the car was delivered as a rolling chassis to Ghia's Turin facility in November 1954, its artisans set about creating a statement that mirrored Wilke's flamboyant sense of style. With its large, egg-crate grille and glitzy brightwork, only the vents down the flanks hinted at the car's competition-inspired origins. This 375 was finished in salmon over anthracite, with a bold chrome spear delineating the contrasting colours; the same shades were carried over into the luxuriously trimmed cabin. In no way was this car subtle.

Unveiled on the Ghia stand at the 1955 Turin Salon, the car was subsequently shipped to the United States, where the North American concessionaire, Luigi Chinetti, borrowed it for that year's New York Auto Show. It remained in Wilke's ownership until his death in 1970. It then passed to his son, along with several other Ferraris; he retained this one-off for a further four years. Subsequent owners have gone to great lengths to preserve rather than restore the car, right down to retaining the original paint and leather upholstery. This dazzling confection is a reminder of Ferrari's bespoke era, when cars were tailored to suit the tastes and whims of their owners, and few customers' tastes were more whimsical than Bob Wilke's.

Ghia's take on the 375 would be the last Ferrari it would ever craft. Towards the end of the 1960s, Alejandro de Tomaso assumed control of the firm: the Argentinian émigré's eponymous supercars would go head-to-head with Ferrari, and briefly outsold the Maranello products in the United States thanks to Ford backing.

Below: Excess all areas. The bold styling was undoubtedly inspired by the flamboyant products emanating from Detroit at the time. The vivid colours and extensive use of chrome brightwork were at odds with most other Ferraris of the period.

Opposite: The orange and slate-grey hues were carried over into the cabin. Remarkably – and commendably – the car has been left largely as it was when it left Ghia's Turin facility: the interior decor is still intact, and the colourful leather has been allowed to mellow.

During the 1950s Ghia was subcontracted to build a series of concept cars for the Chrysler Corporation under the guidance of designer Virgil Exner. Several cues from these show-stoppers can be seen in the America, not least the chrome spear that kicks up behind the doors, and which is used to divide the two contrasting colours.

Left: All the brightwork was hand-formed by Ghia artisans. The once-proud firm had been brought to its knees after the Second World War, and survived by making bicycles. By the mid-1950s it was back to its florid best.

Opposite: The car's original owner, Bob Wilke, often drove the car to race meetings: he was a regular fixture at the Indianapolis 500 and twice sponsored the winning car. Since his death, the car has had few owners and has reputedly covered fewer than 20,000 miles (32,200 km).

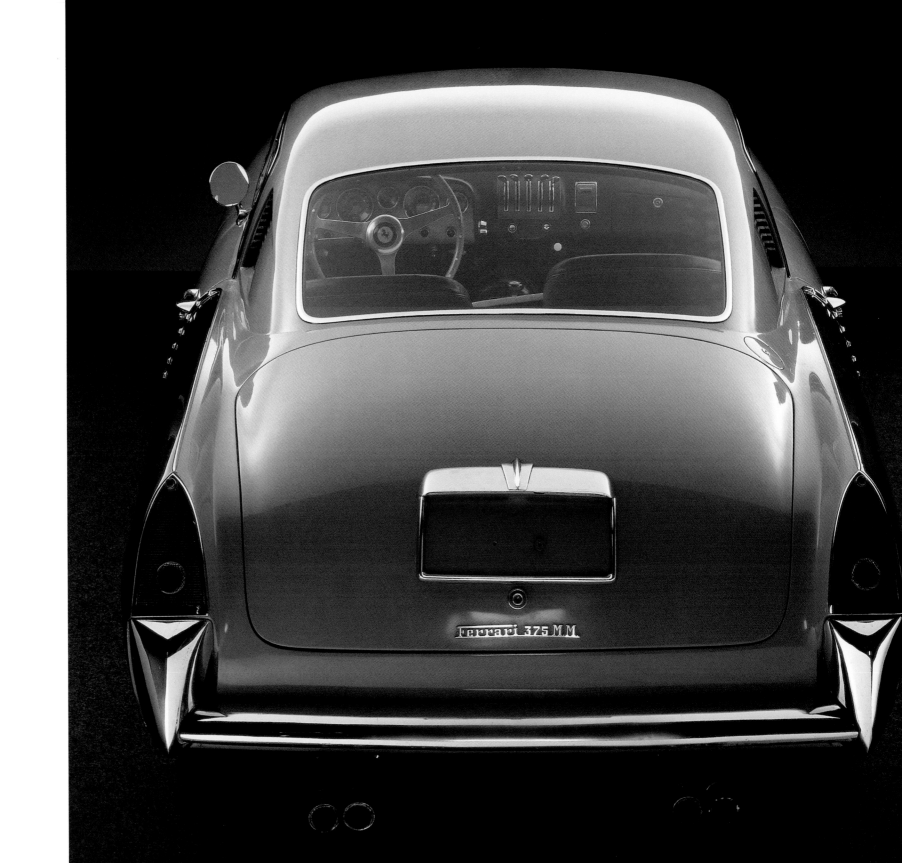

1955 FERRARI 250GT EUROPA BERLINETTA SPECIALE

Continuing Ferrari's early 1950s policy of creating endless variations of the same car, this super-exotic strain of the regular 250GT Europa was built in a small series of just seven units. Four of these featured lightweight aluminium bodies by Pinin Farina that closely followed the look of the 250MM (see p. 52), the remainder bearing altogether more flamboyant outlines. Of these, this example was by far and away the most dramatic. A truly bespoke Ferrari, few cars of this time were as dazzling as this coachbuilt confection – regardless of manufacturer.

This lavish creation bore several highly unusual styling treatments. Some of these would never be repeated on what passed for volume products, while others predicted themes perpetuated for decades. Pinin Farina was clearly given free rein by the first owner, businessman James Murray of Modena: the rear deck design is particularly distinctive. Although first seen a year on from the idiosyncratic one-off 'Agnelli' Ferrari 375MM (see p. 90), here it was integrated into the overall silhouette with greater success. The buttresses, with their downward reverse curves, served to extend the car visually, and in profile lent it the look of a fastback coupé. Viewed from the rear-three-quarter, it was altogether less harmonious. Although not immediately adopted, this styling abstraction would in time appear in refined form on such iconic models as the Dino 206GT (see p. 218).

First shown at the 1955 Turin Salon, this dramatic car was also distinct from its sibling beneath the skin, the anomalous deviation being the wheelbase: 97⅝ in. (2479 mm) rather than the more usual 102⁵⁄₁₆ in. (2598 mm). Three such chassis were made, although the reasoning behind the truncation remains a mystery. Murray didn't retain the car for long; it subsequently headed to the United States, where it was predictably repainted bright red. After appearing in selected historic race meetings, it has more recently been restored to its original silver-grey splendour.

Conceived from the outset as a one-off, this intriguing variation on the 250-series theme was brimful of neat detailing (such as the drilled and polished bonnet pins, above), and showcased some styling cues that would subsequently filter down to production models.

Left: Pinin Farina's stylists were given free rein when producing this car for its original owner, James Murray. The frontal aspect is almost tame by comparison with the rest of the outline, the recessed headlights and ovular grille recess being typical of the Turin firm's Ferrari road cars in period.

Opposite: One-off projects were used as a means of energizing Pinin Farina's designers, while challenging metal works and ultimately – hopefully – pleasing the customer. The rear buttresses on this car were considered controversial when first shown, although this styling aspect was watered down and subsequently applied to future production models, such as the Dino.

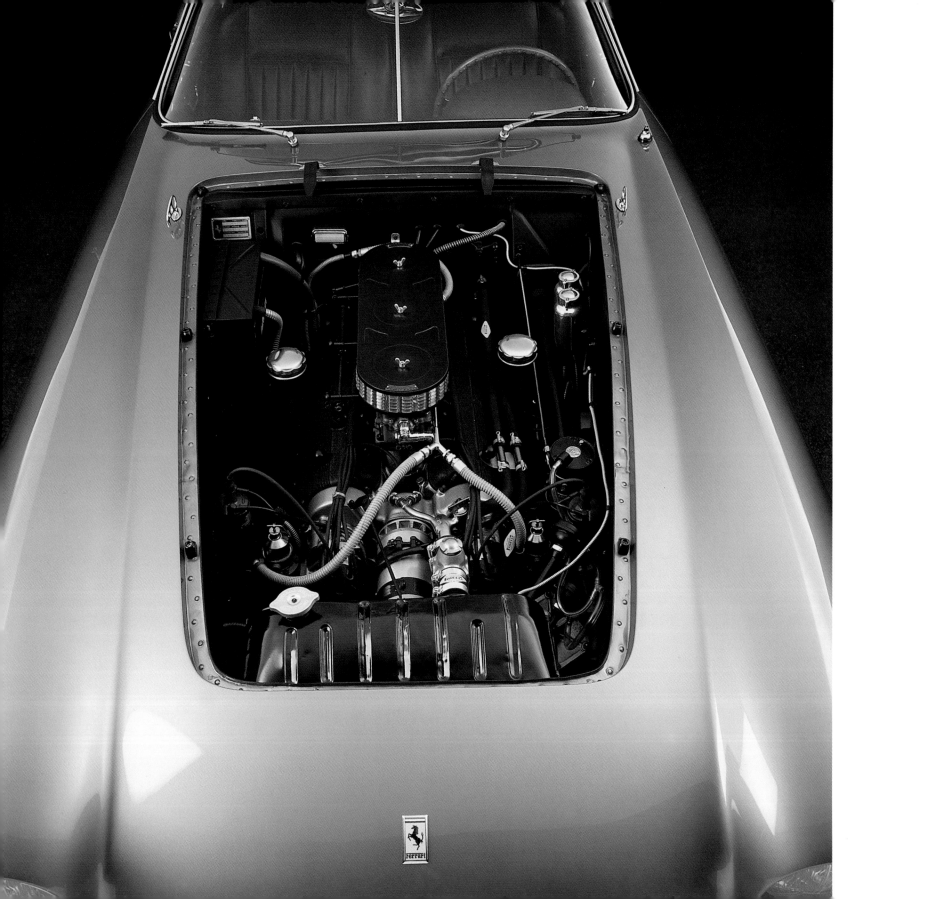

Opposite: The heart of the beast. This glorious, 3-litre V12, fed by three large Weber carburettors, produced in period around 220 bhp at 7000 rpm.

Below: Unusual rear buttresses merge into vestigial tail fins. This wasn't an altogether successful styling feature and appeared at odds with the graceful – and clean – lines fore of the B-pillar.

1955 FERRARI 375MM BERLINETTA

The last of a truly great line, this jet-age coupé marked the denouement of the 375MM, its influence being altogether more far-reaching than can reasonably be expected of a one-off show car. Unveiled at the April 1955 Turin Salon, it predicted styling trends that would gradually filter down to production Ferraris to the end of the decade and beyond. It was a masterpiece of the coachbuilder's art. The Pinin Farina styling house went for broke here and embraced experimentation with renewed gusto for the last of ten 375-series cars clothed by the firm (including competition versions).

The design featured a long wheelbase of 102⅚ in. (2598 mm), a Tipo 102 chassis and the most powerful iteration of Aurelio Lampredi's classic V12 engine. Pinin Farina's brave new world featured a noticeably lower bonnet line and a more compressed grille opening than previous 375MMs, making for a more aggressive look and (theoretically) improved aerodynamic efficiency. This styling treatment was, in part, later borrowed for such models as the 250 Lusso (see p. 187). Especially distinctive were the large louvred vents in the front wings that not only served to hasten the release of heat from under the bonnet, but also acted as a pure styling trick. The forward-leaning vents suggested a sense of motion and also reminded onlookers of the car's competition-led ancestry. Further back, vestigial tail fins appeared, on the probably spurious grounds of aiding stability, but more likely in order to signify weightlessness and flight. The plunging roofline would also become a constant for future Ferrari Berlinettas. This hyper-glamorous GT featured a row of five louvres stacked in the rear window to dissipate cockpit heat, and also to reinforce the sense of speed.

This fabulous creation effectively disappeared from view for decades after its show career ended. Its current owner initiated a restoration and it is once again claiming prizes in concours d'élégance events.

Both under and over the top, this sublime Pinin Farina confection has been extensively and sympathetically restored to its show-car specification of 1955, having at one time been resprayed in a ghastly maroon-and-black two-tone.

Below: The last of the 375MMs. The dramatic, swept-back outline hints at the car's competition-inspired ancestry, the vestigial tail fins imbuing a sense of flight.

Opposite: During the car's restoration, much of the original cabin was reinstated, including the original instruments. Other items were precisely replicated, right down to the ribbed floor matting.

The Plexiglas rear screen is the original item. The small louvres are in place to help dissipate cockpit heat, although their effectiveness is debatable.

1956 FERRARI 250GTZ BERLINETTA

Zagato is justifiably venerated for its coachbuilding artistry, the Milan firm having created several landmark designs since its inception in 1919. On the flipside, it has routinely proved capable of gaping credibility chasms. Unfortunately, this famous *carrozzeria* tends to lose the plot whenever called upon to body a Ferrari, having clothed its first in 1949 with typically idiosyncratic results. Fortunately, the car photographed here is a rare exception: it's exquisite.

One of two 250-series cars built in sequence (Zagato bodied five in total), it was outwardly similar to its sibling but differed in intended purpose. Its sister car was headed trackside and won several sports-car classes; this one was destined for an altogether more cosseted existence, if only initially. Commissioned by a wealthy Milanese, Vladimiro Galluzzi, at a cost of 900,000 lire (on top of the 3 million lire charged by Ferrari for the rolling chassis), it featured such totemic Zagato styling treatments as the distinctive 'double-bubble' roof. Becoming something of a show queen, it trotted before judges at the prestigious Cortina d'Ampezzo and Campione d'Italia concours events, but, just to prove the car's duality of character, Galluzi entered it in the Dolomite Gold Cup in July 1956 and finished second in class (its sister car – a week apart in age – won outright). At the end of the year, the construction boss sold the car to Scuderia Sant'Ambroeus, which in turn moved it on to a Genoa car dealer, who installed Luigi Taramazzo to race the car. On 1 September 1957, Taramazzo steered it to first overall in the Garessio–San Bernardo hillclimb, and the following week placed third in the XI Coppa Intereuropa at Monza.

Sold to the United States in 1960, this fabulous machine passed through several owners – one buying and selling it five times over – before heading to Switzerland and then to Mexico. More recently it has been comprehensively restored and currently lives in a private Beverly Hills collection.

Zagato has clothed several Ferraris, with varying degrees of success. This fabulous creation is undoubtedly the Milan firm's best yet, imbued with beauty and such quirks as the 'double-bubble' roof.

Above: Zagato bodied its first Ferrari in 1949, and was justifiably renowned for its overtly sporting outlook. This example was conceived as a road car, but predictably ended up being campaigned. Its sister car was the class of the field in Italian sports-car races in 1956.

Opposite: The cabin is stylish without being clichéd, and mirrors the car's colour scheme. The roof humps supposedly freed up additional headroom for taller drivers while affording additional strength to the bodyshell.

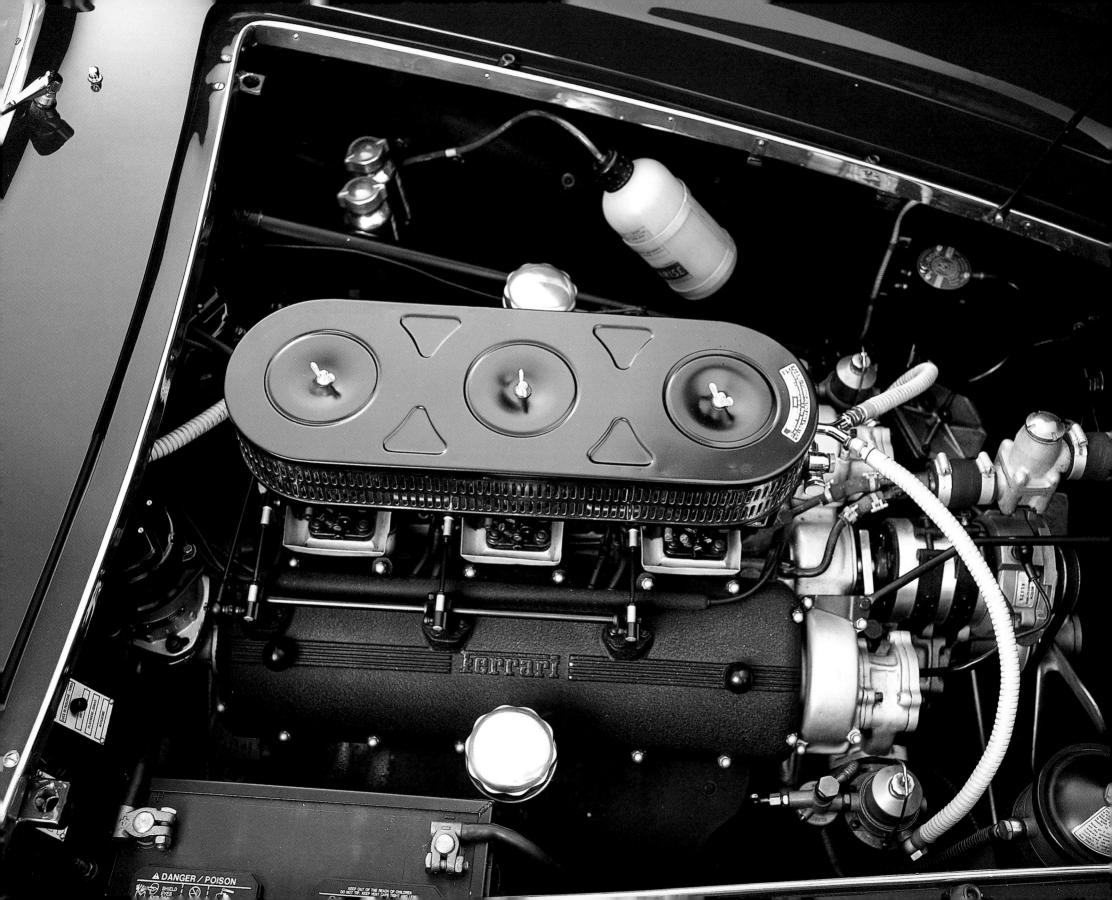

Opposite: The classic V12 provides a stirring soundtrack. The engine, chassis and running gear were supplied new by Ferrari for a thumping 3 million lire.

Right: Zagato's coachwork added an extra 900,000 lire to the end price. Since its restoration in the early 2000s, the car has been a regular on the concours d'élégance circuit, and has also completed the Mille Miglia road race retrospective.

1956 FERRARI 860 MONZA

With only a short-lived racing career behind it, it's easy to forget that the 860 Monza belongs among more exalted competition Ferraris. But this would be to do the model a disservice. This achingly pretty machine was instrumental in the *scuderia* securing the 1956 World Sportscar Championship. This car was essentially a stopgap while Ferrari set about developing a replacement for the 750 Monza. The firm's backroom boffins sought to increase the capacity of the existing four-cylinder engine from 3 litres to 3432 cc. Producing 310 bhp at a heady 7200 rpm, this would prove to have the largest displacement of any four-cylinder unit ever made by Ferrari. Mounted in the regular 750 Monza chassis, and bearing the familiar Scaglietti outline, just three of these cars were made.

This particular example kicked off the factory team's 1956 programme with victory in the Sebring 12 Hours for Juan Manuel Fangio and Eugenio Castellotti. It was subsequently sold to the influential California Ferrari dealer and occasional racer John von Neumann, who alternated driving duties on the West Coast with future Formula One world champion Phil Hill and Richie Ginther for the remainder of the season and into 1957. After only sporadic outings in 1958, it was sold to Jerry Baker, who installed Lew Florence for eight events during the following season. Florence won four and placed second in two more. In the 1960s the car became part of the famed Collection Mas du Clos in France, where it remained until 1987 before passing to the Musée de l'Automobiliste on the Côte d'Azur. Subsequent owners included the former Renault Formula One team boss (and Ferrari F40 race entrant) Jean Sage. In 2006 this fabulous sports-racer was sold at auction for $3.5 million – not bad for a temporary fix.

Though essentially an expedient quick fix while a new car was readied, the fearsome 860 Monza deserves veneration. It served Ferrari well, helping the *scuderia* attain the 1956 World Sportscar Championship crown.

Aside from being blisteringly quick, the 860 Monza was also exquisitely beautiful, the outline being the work of Scaglietti, which also produced the aluminium bodywork.

Opposite: One of only three 860s ever made, this car won the 1956 Sebring 12 Hours with the driver pairing of Juan Manuel Fangio and Eugenio Castellotti. It subsequently found great success on the West Coast of America with future Formula One world champion Phil Hill.

Right: With the largest displacement of any four-cylinder engine ever fitted to a Ferrari, this 3.5-litre monster produced over 300 bhp at a dizzying 7200 rpm.

1956 FERRARI 250GT BERLINETTA 'TOUR DE FRANCE'

It was an event that pushed competitors beyond endurance. Starting in Nice, and ending five days and 3345 miles (5383 km) later in Paris, the Tour de France was not for the faint of heart. A true test of resilience and adaptability, this event became a Ferrari benefit during the 1950s and proved beyond all doubt the durability of the Maranello cars on road, rally and hillclimb stages. It was commonplace for three-quarters of the entrants to drop out before the finish. Only the toughest of the tough could go the distance; one such was Alfonso Antonio Vicente Eduardo Angel Blas Francisco de Borja Cabeza de Vaca y Leighton, the 17th Marquis de Portago (known to his friends as 'Fon'). This English-born Spanish nobleman won the event in 1956, presaging a four-year winning streak for the marque.

Such was Ferrari's dominance in the event that the long-wheelbase (102$\frac{5}{16}$ in./2598 mm) 250-series Berlinettas have long since been referred to by the Tour de France moniker (or simply 'TdF'). Each chassis received coachbuilt bodies, usually by Scaglietti to a Pinin Farina design, although Zagato of Milan also clothed five typically idiosyncratic coupés (see p. 120). Even among what passed for production models, no two cars ever looked alike, with subtle differences between headlight arrangement (exposed or inset behind Perspex) and in the profile of the rear screen, early cars being modelled along similar lines to the 250MM (see p. 52). By 1959 the chassis had been shortened to 94½ in. (2400 mm), the one common feature being the iconic 3-litre Colombo V12 engine.

The Tour de France was one of the great road-race Ferraris. When it passed the baton to the even more sublime 250GT SWB (see p. 155) in 1959, its legendary status was already assured.

One of the truly great Ferraris, each TdF nonetheless differed in detail, with the headlights sometimes recessed behind Perspex cowls.

Below: Based on a chassis with a 94½-in. (2400-mm) wheelbase, the Tour de France was supremely graceful; Scaglietti bodied most of the cars, to a Pinin Farina brief.

Opposite: The TdF's cabin was functional, as befitted a race-bred racer. It was comfortable, too, as is to be expected of a long-distance competition tool.

Until it was usurped by the 250SWB, the Tour de France was the car of choice for endurance drivers, scoring overall wins and class honours in most major races, rallies and hillclimbs of the period.

1956 FERRARI 250GT SERIES 1 CABRIOLET

It was a car for the elite: nominally a production model but in essence a series of egregiously expensive one-offs tailored to suit the whims and fancies of individual customers. Those fortunate enough to be able to buy one of these exquisite machines as they were built included royalty, industry tycoons and the obligatory beautiful people: Prince Ali Kahn (husband of Rita Hayworth) had one, as did Prince Mohamed Al Faisal of Saudi Arabia, racing gadabout Porfirio Rubirosa (see Mondial 500, p. 85), youthful motor-sport team principal Count Giovanni Volpi di Misurata and the dashing (and tragic) Formula One star Peter Collins. Just forty Cabriolets – including four prototypes – were made, making it one of the most exclusive open Ferraris ever made. And one of the most coveted.

Inspiration for this limited-series run came from a custom-bodied 250GT penned by Mario Boano and shown at the 1956 Geneva Salon. Intrigued by this open roadster, Battista 'Pinin' Farina refined the proportions and debuted his own take at the same venue a year on. Built for Collins, then a much-loved member of Ferrari's works race team, the show car was dazzling, rakish even, although some of the detailing caused puzzlement. On the driver's side, the doors were cutaway in the style of contemporary British sports cars, but the passenger-side door was conventionally straight-edged. Production cars were more conformist, although detail differences ensured that no two were ever alike: some featured front bumperettes, others full-width items, while a handful of late-model examples had exposed headlights.

Unique to all was the familiar 2953-cc Colombo V12, with output varying between 220 and 240 bhp at a vocal 7000 rpm. The factory claimed a top speed of 135 mph (217 km/h) – although no independent tests ever verified this – and a 0–60 mph (0–96.5 km/h) time of 7.1 seconds. With the introduction of the Series II edition of 1959 came a more standardized Cabriolet that, while fabulous in its own right, could never match its predecessor's rarefied glamour.

Although not one of the more fondly remembered Ferraris, the 250PF was once one of the most exclusive sports cars on the planet, owned by royalty, movie stars and assorted glitterati.

A truly glamorous machine, the first-generation Cabriolet was arguably the prettier of the two series. Later cars had full-width front bumpers, which slightly diluted the front-end styling.

1957 FERRARI 250 TESTA ROSSA

It was a disaster of epic proportions, and in a roundabout way it resulted in another period of Ferrari dominance. Following the 1955 tragedy at Le Mans, in which Pierre Levegh's Mercedes-Benz was launched into the crowd after tapping the back of Lance Macklin's Austin-Healey, killing eighty-two racegoers, regulations were gradually implemented to curb speeds. For 1958, the World Sportscar Championship had its engine capacity capped at 3 litres. Ferrari was ready for just such an eventuality.

The *scuderia* had already produced a four-cylinder Testa Rossa ('Red Head', so named after the engine's scarlet camshaft covers), which raced in 1956 and 1957. A 3-litre V12 prototype was then entered in the 1957 Nürburgring 1000 km race, a second car being readied for that year's Le Mans 24 Hours: the public debut for the new – and wild – 'pontoon fender' body style.

Once *the* dominant force in sports-car racing, the original Testa Rossa was as visually daring as it was fast.

Described by coachbuilder Sergio Scaglietti as a 'Formula One car with fenders', the distinctive cut-outs around the front wheels were in place to help cool the brakes, although the works cars subsequently reverted to more conventional bodywork. This was apparently done at the behest of drivers who believed the cutaway shape rendered the cars aerodynamically unstable at speed, but this has never been publicly verified. All nineteen customer cars retained the controversial styling.

The 1958 season would prove a walkover for the red cars. Kicking off at Buenos Aires, Argentina, in late January, Peter Collins and Phil Hill shared the winning car, the duo teaming up two months later to conquer the Sebring 12 Hours. Luigi Musso came out on top in May's Targa Florio road race with Olivier Gendebien, the latter joining Hill to seal the manufacturers' title with victory in June's Le Mans 24 Hours. Of the five championship rounds that year, the Testa Rossa failed to prevail only in the Nürburgring 1000 km, where Stirling Moss and Jack Brabham won for Aston Martin. Ferraris took the following four places. Such dominance in motor sport has rarely been repeated.

Opposite: Built for competition, the Testa Rossa was nonetheless a road-going machine. This is reflected in the cabin, which lacks the stark functionality of Ferrari's later race-only sports-prototypes.

Below: This is arguably the best view of the 'Red Head', an awe-inspiring creation bodied – and penned – by Scaglietti.

M. MARCOTULLI

Possibly the most dramatic sports-racer of the 1950s, the 'pontoon fender' Testa Rossa was also the most easily recognizable. Some drivers claimed that the cutaway wings upset the car's aerodynamic balance, but this has never been proven.

1958 FERRARI 250GT CALIFORNIA

One of the most desirable Ferrari road cars ever made, the California represented yet another attempt at exploiting North America's susceptibility to the lure of Italian exotica. The brainchild of John von Neumann, Ferrari's influential West Coast distributor whose clientele numbered most of Hollywood's glitterati, the car was initially conceived as a convertible version of the Tour de France (see p. 133). Using the same 102⁵/₁₆-in. (2598-mm) Tipo 508C chassis and a 3-litre Colombo V12 engine, it ended up becoming much more than just a chop top conversion. In what was essentially a reclothing exercise, the sublime styling was the work of Scaglietti, although Pinin Farina is widely believed to have had some input. Bodied in steel, save for the aluminium doors, bonnet and boot lid, the California was a work of singular beauty. The prototype was completed in late 1957, but the first production example wasn't delivered to Ferrari's North American concessionaire, Luigi Chinetti, until June of the following year.

Perhaps *the* most glamorous Ferrari roadster ever made, the California was predictably created with North America – and the West Coast in particular – in mind. The beautiful people flocked to buy one; they still do.

Proving moderately popular in its intended market, some fifty-one cars were made before the model received upgrades in line with the 250GT SWB. The most notable changes were a truncated 94½-in. (2400-mm) wheelbase and a power hike to around 260 bhp at 7000 rpm. Top speed was reputedly 145 mph (233 km/h), with the 0–60 mph (0–96.5 km/h) sprint taking a whisker over six seconds. No two cars were ever truly alike, and typically there were two distinct headlight treatments – Perspex-enshrouded or exposed. Production continued until early 1963, by which time a further fifty-six examples had been completed.

Having latterly gained a level of pop-culture fame for its appearance in the 1986 comedy *Ferris Bueller's Day Off* (although the two cars used in the movie were replicas), the 250GT California is among the most easily identifiable of all classic Ferraris.

Above: The California's beautifully proportioned outline was the work of Scaglietti, although Pinin Farina is reputed to have lent its input. Predictably, each car differed in the details.

Opposite: The simple but chic cabin, the speedometer and rev counter the driver's main point of focus. Supplementary gauges are sited in the centre of the fascia.

Even with the roof in place, the California still looks elegant. The canvas top, however, can be quite a challenge to erect.

1959   FERRARI 250GT SWB

This fabulous GT blurred the line between road and racing car like few others, its duality of character exemplified by Stirling Moss's efforts during the 1960 Tourist Trophy race. Lapping Goodwood en route to a commanding victory aboard Rob Walker's fully road-equipped version, he whiled away the time twiddling the radio dials between music stations and Raymond Baxter's live race commentary for the BBC. Had Moss been inclined to do so, there was no reason why the future knight couldn't have driven home in the car afterwards.

The model was first seen at the 1959 Paris Salon. Its nomenclature referred to its shorter wheelbase: 94½ in. (2400 mm), some 7¾ in. (198 mm) shorter than preceding 250-series models; this truncation surgery in theory improved cornering agility. The SWB's other novelty was its adoption of Dunlop disc brakes – the first time for a Ferrari (and a full six years after Jaguar pioneered their use at Le Mans). Offered in numerous guises, most of these 3-litre V12 beauties were sold in Lusso (luxury) trim, with steel bodywork (aluminium doors, bonnet and boot), leather upholstery and detuned 240 bhp engines. For the racer, there was the option of all-aluminium coachwork and an extra 40 bhp. Hottest of them all, though, were the SEFAC (Scuderia Enzo Ferrari Auto Corse) 'Hot Rods' with monstrous Weber carburettors and gossamer-thin panels.

The SWB was among the last truly handmade Ferraris; its other major draw was its styling. The cars were designed at Pininfarina (one word from 1959), and built by Scaglietti, and it's unlikely that any two were ever identical dimensionally. There wasn't a single jarring line, unsurprising in a product from a design house then at the height of its powers. Around 165 cars are believed to have been made, with survivors being highly prized.

A brilliant road car and an even better competition tool, the 250GT SWB remains an icon in Ferrari lore. As motor sport and road-car development diverged, it was arguably the last truly great Ferrari road-going racer.

Below: Leaving aside its performance capabilities, the SWB earned legendary status in Ferrari history as much for its outer beauty. Another Pininfarina confection, its perfectly proportioned outline was inspired by function but was breathtaking nevertheless.

Opposite: It's unusual to see an SWB in 'Fly Yellow', the body-coloured dashboard adding a flash of brightness to the otherwise no-nonsense cabin. Predictably, Enrico Nardi's trademark wood-rim, alloy-spoked steering wheel dominates proceedings.

Scaglietti clothed the SWB in aluminium for racers, or mostly out of steel for pure road cars. The model's passing marked the beginning of the end for Ferrari's coachbuilt era, as volume products began to take precedence.

Left: Minimal frontal overhang and a limited use of brightwork lent the nose area a clean, uncluttered look. The front bumpers were often removed on competition versions.

Opposite: The fabulous V12 powerplant was offered in a 240-bhp road-car specification, or in a 280-bhp configuration for competition use.

1959 FERRARI 400 SUPERAMERICA CABRIOLET

The 1950s witnessed a barrage of hyper-glamorous Ferraris, all built in very small numbers for the beautiful people, but none could top this devilish device for eye-watering extravagance. From 1959 to 1964, the most powerful production car to wear the Cavallino Rampante was the 400 Superamerica. First presented at the November 1959 Turin Salon, it married a 4.9-litre V12 engine, designed by Aurelio Lampredi and derived from Grand Prix cars, with a shortened 250GT chassis, on to which was fitted Pininfarina coachwork.

The Cabriolet version was announced at the 1961 Geneva Salon, and since Ferrari had not yet fully embraced mass production techniques, each car was different in detail. However, it was royally upstaged by the new Jaguar E-type, which rendered the Ferrari a mite sober – if only in appearance – by comparison. North America was the target audience (witness the less than subtle nomenclature), but ultimately the car proved a flop: U.S. customers didn't rush to embrace the open version, preferring instead the existing 250GT Cabriolet. From 1962, a longer wheelbase model – the Series II – was offered, but this similarly failed to find favour, and just ten Superamerica Cabriolets were crafted by Pininfarina (plus an eleventh by Scaglietti) of both types.

Marrying a Grand Prix car-derived engine with bespoke, tailored bodywork, the 400 Superamerica was only ever going to be patronized by the elite. Nonetheless, it still bombed in its intended marketplace – the West Coast of America.

The example shown here was completed in March 1961 and trumpeted on Pininfarina's stand at the model's Geneva debut. Originally finished in metallic ivory, it was subsequently sold to a Milanese doctor who returned the car to the *carrozzeria* to be resprayed in Blue Antille Savid and retrimmed. Ironically for a model that singularly failed in its intended marketplace, the 400 Superamerica is now highly sought after, this car belonging to a prominent New York-based Ferrari collector.

Opposite: Despite its asking price, the Superamerica was less overtly showy than many Ferraris of the day. Very much built to special order, it wasn't a huge success, with customers preferring the regular production 250GT model.

Below: With the rare factory hardtop in place, the Superamerica is arguably even better looking. It's doubtful, however, that many owners ever took up the optional extra.

Below: Pininfarina often took styling themes established on exotica and reworked them on more proletarian cars. Certainly the rear-end treatment here was applied to Fiats and Peugeots.

Opposite: The magnificent Aurelio Lampredi-conceived V12 produced over 300 bhp and was the most powerful unit then offered in a non-competition Ferrari.

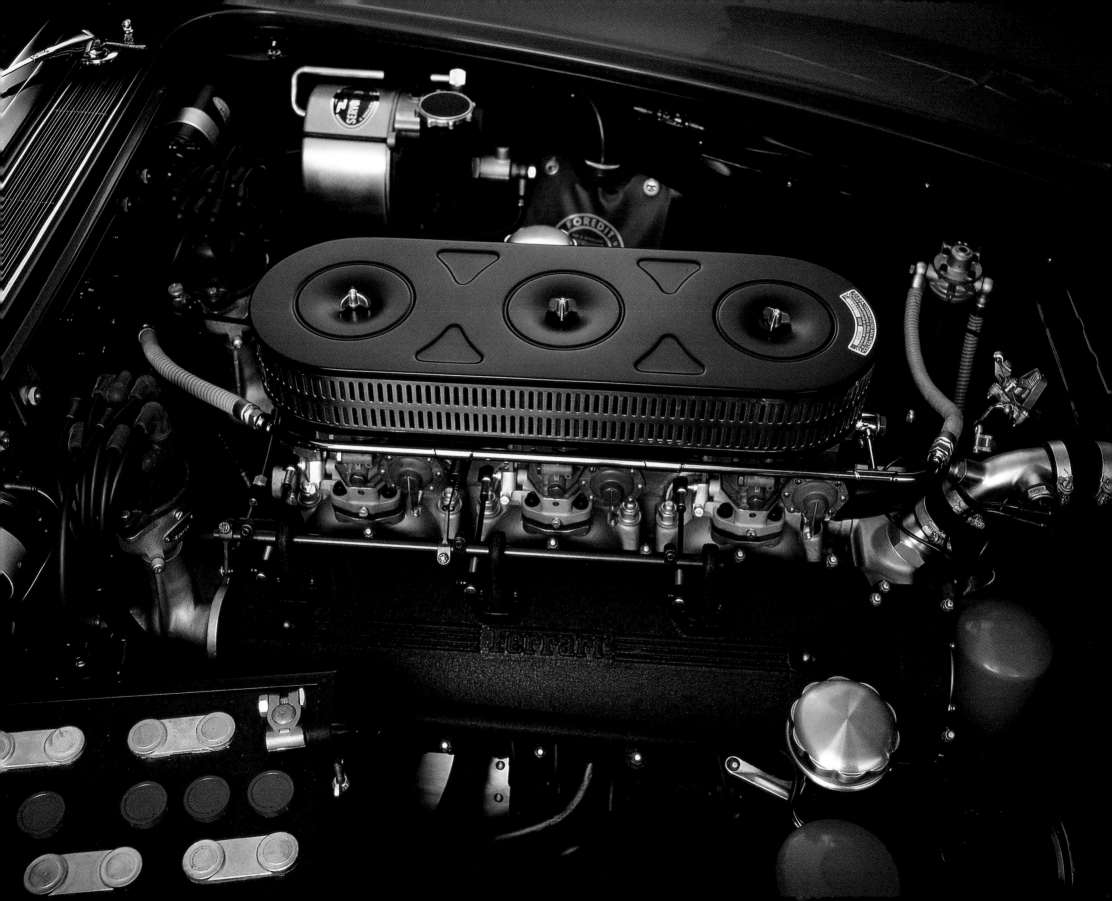

1960 FERRARI 250GTE

By the late 1950s Enzo Ferrari began to realize the value of building road cars in volume. They provided much-needed revenue to fund his team's participation in an ever-expanding programme of motor racing. First seen as a course car at the June 1960 Le Mans 24 Hours, and officially launched at October's Paris Salon, this delightful coupé represented the marque's first serious attempt at anything approaching mass production. Constructed at a rate of between five and six cars per week until 1963, it was easily the most successful model up to that time.

Borrowing heavily from earlier 250-series cars, the GTE retained the classic 3-litre Colombo V12 fed by three Weber carburettors, tuned to produce around 240 bhp at 7000 rpm, and mounted in the standard 102 5/16-in. (2598-mm) Tipo 508 chassis. However, the engine was moved further forward to create greater cabin space, which, together with wider front and rear tracks, allowed for the addition of rear seats. Predictably, Pininfarina was employed to produce an outline, the handsome GTE being bodied in steel, except for aluminium doors, bonnet and boot lid.

In late 1962 the Series II edition was announced. This had mainly interior-led detail revisions, with the final iteration – predictably dubbed the Series III – arriving at the following year's Geneva Salon. Alterations centred largely on the repositioning of driving lights and the reprofiling of the rear wings. Some 950 were made, of all types, before the arrival of its replacement, the 330GT 2+2. Except that wasn't altogether the end of the story. Pininfarina had a contract with Ferrari to supply 1000 GTE bodyshells over a fixed period. In order to honour the commitment, a further fifty cars were made as the 330 America – a 250GTE hull but with a 300-bhp Tipo 109 V12 engine. Tragically, a great many GTEs have latterly been sacrificed to make 250GTO replicas and other fake racers, with as many as 10 per cent of total production being butchered.

A hugely successful volume-seller, the GTE's fortunes have latterly taken a dip, with many being used as the basis for replicas of more exalted Ferrari racing cars.

Left: The 'Colombo' V12 was detuned for this application, although the GTE could still exceed 140 mph (225 km/h) overall – heady stuff for the early 1960s.

Opposite: The GTE's beautifully proportioned outline was the work of Pininfarina. This 'family' Ferrari – the two rear seats were at best suitable only for use by children – was a big car, but its bulk is expertly disguised.

1961 FERRARI 400 SUPERAMERICA 'COUPÉ AERODYNAMICA'

This fabulous machine broke cover at the January 1960 Brussels Salon, and the timing of its debut seems to have taken on an extra resonance in hindsight. During a decade that would witness standardization across the board for production road cars, not to mention Fiat's assumption of control at Ferrari, the latest incarnation of the Superamerica effectively marked the beginning of the end for Ferrari's 'boutique era'.

Distinct from the previous Superamerica (see p. 162), this latest strain did away with evolutionary threads, being powered by a significantly smaller 3967-cc V12. Stylistically, the first few cars broke no new ground, being rehashes of the outgoing edition, but a new and dramatic design language was established in time for the November 1960 Turin Salon. Pininfarina's Superfast II show car laid out the template for the production Superamerica 'Coupé Aerodynamica', which was further refined in detail before small-scale manufacture began early in 1961. An uncompromising statement of aerodynamic intent, the outline resembled an aircraft wing: rounded at the front and tapered to a point at the rear.

Pininfarina's fabulous outline for this super-coupé borrowed heavily from aeronautical design: the 'Aerodynamica' nomenclature was more than just PR puff.

This example – the fifth to be built – was extra special, having been made for hotelier and motor museum owner Bill Harrah. Notoriously particular about his cars, he was reputedly disappointed by the Superamerica's performance (around 340 bhp at 7000 rpm) and thus had Bill Rudd at Modern Classic Motors of Reno reassemble the engine with forged pistons and monstrous carburettors while boring it out to 4590 cc. In this form, *Road & Track*'s Dean Batchelor recorded 150 mph (241 km/h) before running out of road while convinced that 185 mph (298 km/h) was possible. Summarizing his experiences with this extraordinary GT, he wrote: 'At the risk of sounding like a Ferrari press agent, we can honestly say that to own a car such as this would be the ultimate in automotive satisfaction.' As testimonials go, that's pretty emphatic.

Although perhaps not conventionally pretty, the 'Coupé Aerodynamica' was nothing if not extreme. The rear wheels were semi-enclosed to avoid aerodynamic drag, while the rear end was tapered like an aircraft wing.

Opposite: The headlights were recessed behind Perspex cowls so as not to interrupt the airflow; the tusk-like bumperettes were in place to protect the vulnerable nose.

Right: The fabulous cabin featured a speedometer that read up to 300 km/h (186 mph). This particular example was independently road-tested by the influential *Road & Track* magazine, which believed that this heady velocity was indeed achievable.

1962 FERRARI 250GTO

In motor racing, you're never a cheat until you get caught. Or, as some (mostly British) rivals routinely put it, you're Ferrari. For 1962, the CSI (Commission Sportive Internationale) decreed that the World Sportscar Championship would be replaced by a series for GT cars. In one of the most audacious acts of chicanery perpetuated in top-flight competition, Ferrari took a more lateral approach to rule interpretation and built an out-and-out racer instead: the fabulous 250GTO.

The rules stated that one hundred cars needed to be constructed to appease homologation requirements. Between December 1961 and May 1964, Ferrari made just thirty-nine GTOs (the 'O' preposterously standing for 'Omologato'), the *scuderia* claiming that it was merely an evolution of the 250GT SWB, of which the requisite number had already been built. Aided and abetted by race organizers wanting Ferraris on their grids, this scheme worked.

One of the most famous cars of all time, and the most coveted, the 250GTO was a flagrant cheat as a racing car, but a magnificent one nonetheless.

Though based on the existing 250GT SWB tubular-steel chassis, the GTO was longer, lower, wider and 551 lb (250 kg) lighter, with the existing Lampredi 3-litre V12 being tuned to produce 295 bhp. During the three years the model was actively campaigned, the GTO won twenty out of twenty-eight World Championship rounds, finishing second in fifteen and third in nine. Ferrari's smoke-and-mirrors approach had worked, but when it subsequently tried to pull off the same ruse with its 250LM (blatantly a sports-racer), the Maranello squad received a rude awakening from once-burned regulators: the 250GTO had made a delicious mockery of the men in suits.

Yet for all its on-track glory, this awe-inspiring racing car is deified more for its bestial elegance – the prototype was chopped and changed by engineer Giotto Bizzarrini and coachbuilder Scaglietti until it looked 'presentable' – and latter-day price tags. One example was sold for $15 million to a Japanese collector in the late 1980s. The knock-on effect witnessed several 'lesser' Ferraris being tragically sliced and diced to create replicas.

Left: A low frontal area and recessed headlights helped the GTO cleave the air. Although aerodynamics were still something of a black art in the early 1960s, this was a much sleeker car than the 250GT SWB it replaced.

Opposite: Despite being a road car – and an accomplished one at that – the GTO was every inch the racer, as evinced by the cabin and its lack of carpeting and door cards: they added weight.

For a car that wasn't styled so much as left to evolve, the GTO remains one of the most extraordinary acts of automotive artistry ever perpetrated. Engineer Giotto Bizzarrini and coachbuilder Scaglietti whittled the outline until it looked presentable; beauty was a happy by-product.

Opposite: The glorious 'Lampredi' V12, a wonder of mechanical splendour, perfectly reflected the car's outer glory. When tuned for races, the mighty powerplant put out almost 300 bhp.

Above: Cut-outs behind the rear wheels helped to cool the brakes, while the raised-lip spoiler atop the cropped tail provided downforce to keep the car planted on the road.

1962   FERRARI 250 LUSSO

The acme of Ferrari's over-achieving 250-series line, the GT Berlinetta Lusso had an alluring outline that represented a major break away from Pininfarina's 1950s 'cubist period'. Although ostensibly designing a road car – 'Lusso' means 'luxury' – the Turin styling house produced a vision of gorgeousness fused with design cues cherry-picked from the marque's recent competition endeavours. The roofline was pure 330 Le Mans coupé, the shark nose a nod to contemporaneous sports- and Formula One racers.

Debuting at the 1962 Paris Salon (although the Lusso was late arriving), this car exhausted the supply of superlatives available to motoring writers. After a marathon drive from Milan to Le Mans and back again, aristocrat and former racer Count Giovanni 'Johnny' Lurani raved in *Auto Italiano Sport*: 'the 250GT Berlinetta thoroughly confirmed its right as the most exceptional high-performance sports car in existence – the very best in the world.'

Borrowing its independent double wishbone and coil-sprung front suspension from the 250GTO (the rear end features a live axle on semi-elliptic springs with trailing arms and a Watts linkage), it also featured the same 3-litre V12. The engine was detuned to a more modest 250 bhp, although its biggest deviation was its repositioning several inches further forward to free up cockpit space. Revisionists claim that this move spoiled the car's handling, but it was praised at the time. Bodied in steel (with aluminium only for the bonnet, door skins and boot) by Scaglietti, the car's 2912-lb (1321-kg) heft blunted performance by comparison with its racy brethren. Nonetheless, the Lusso could still reach 100 mph (161 km/h) from a standstill in seventeen seconds, with a top speed – if the factory claims were to be believed – of 145 mph (233 km/h). During its two-year life, around 350 were made, of which just twenty-three were in right-hand-drive.

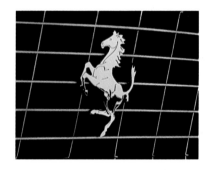

Occupying the middle ground between the racier 250-series competition cars and the larger 2+2 'family' Ferraris, the Lusso borrowed its foundations from the GTO, albeit with its engine moved further forward.

For a firm with such a rich back catalogue, Pininfarina's outline for the Lusso remains one of its greatest ever. There isn't a single jarring line, only beautifully realized – and emblematic – cues taken from its competition brethren and reworked into one hugely desirable whole.

Left: The cabin was equally a masterpiece, with heavily bolstered bucket seats trimmed in leather. The instrument arrangement was unique to the model, while the quilted rear deck featured retaining straps for luggage.

Opposite: The cropped rear end is a study in understatement, and mirrored similar treatments found on other models in the range. All 350 or so Lussos were nominally the same, with Ferrari moving ever closer to standardizing output.

In profile, the Lusso is unencumbered by unnecessary styling additions; no vents or louvres, nothing to blight the picture. The slim pillars and wrap-around rear screen afford panoramic, all-round vision.

1964   FERRARI 275GTB

Few cars can eclipse the beauty of this creation by Aldo Bravarone. The Pininfarina stylist created a perfectly balanced outline that still captivates: the car remains among the most desirable production Ferraris ever made, and beauty arbiters in the motoring media routinely cite it as being a landmark in marque lore. All the more remarkable, then, that the 275-series remained in production for only a relatively short period of time – 1964 to 1968 – with several different subspecies to choose from. A favourite of the celebrity set, the car's customers included the movie stars Steve McQueen, Alain Delon and James Coburn.

Distinct from previous Ferrari road cars, the 275 was the first to feature independent rear suspension, along with a five-speed transaxle. Its twin-cam V12 engine was a direct relation of that found in the back of the 250LM sports-racer. Crafted by Scaglietti, the bodies were hand-formed from steel, except for the aluminium doors, bonnet and boot lid. Predictably, an all-aluminium shell was available as an option. Entering production in October 1964, and retrospectively – and unofficially – referred to as the Series Short Nose, it was replaced twelve months later by the Series II iteration, which had a longer, more pointed nose to alleviate front-end lift at speed. In January 1966 a new and improved chassis was initiated, with a new quad-cam engine the following October at the Paris Salon. The most obvious physical difference was a prominent bonnet bulge to accommodate the carburettors' air cleaner.

Though ostensibly a road car, three distinct motor sport-orientated variations were made. The best result for the Competizione editions occurred in the 1966 Le Mans 24 Hours, when the Anglo-American pairing of Piers Courage and Roy Pike won their class and finished eighth overall for the British Maranello Concessionaires team. In doing so, they upheld Ferrari's honour, as theirs was the only example of the marque to finish the endurance classic that year.

Replacing the 250 Lusso was always going to be a challenge, but Ferrari and the reliably terrific Pininfarina pulled it off with the 275GTB, arguably the most desirable GT car either has ever produced.

Opposite: Inside, the cabin was pure jet-set, with deep bucket seats and a three-spoke steering wheel. Every detail, from the spring-loaded ashtray to the yellow-on-black Ferrari insignia on the horn push, was carefully considered.

Right: Graceful yet muscular. The dramatically arced fastback roof gently melds into the aggressive haunches before tapering into a sweetly cropped tail.

Opposite: The unheralded Aldo Bravarone was responsible for the GTB's outline. Each car was a coupé, save for a batch of ten NART (North American Racing Team) convertibles.

Right: The marvellous V12 was an evolution of the unit found in the rear of the Le Mans-winning 250LM sports-racer, and was routinely upgraded during the GTB's four-year lifespan.

Although ostensibly a road car, several examples (with varying degrees of modification) were entered into competition. This example was campaigned by the Swiss team Scuderia Filipinetti.

Some seventeen all-alloy-bodied GTBs are believed to have been made with competition use in mind, the high point for the model being class honours in the 1966 Le Mans 24 Hours – the only finish for a Ferrari at that year's French endurance classic.

1967   FERRARI 330P4

Arguably the most beautiful sports-racing car ever made, this vision of gorgeousness represented a final hurrah for curvature before aerodynamic and packaging requirements prompted ever more geometric designs. From an era not entirely lacking in beautiful cars, this one was produced by eye and intuition, with artisans at Piero Drogo's Carrozzeria Sports Cars concern hand-forming the aluminium bodywork that swooped and pitched with sensuous harmony around the ellipsoidal windscreen. Not even the air intake ducts or cooling louvres blighted the picture.

Made in Spider (open) or Berlinetta (closed) forms, the P4 was Ferrari's rejoinder to Ford's GT40, which had humbled the *scuderia* at the 1966 Le Mans 24 Hours. Visually similar to the outgoing P3, it nonetheless differed greatly. Power came from a mid-mounted, 36-valve 4-litre V12, related, if only in part, to a Formula One engine designed by Franco Rocchi that had first appeared at the 1966 Italian Grand Prix. Unusually for the marque, this gem featured British Lucas fuel-injection rather than regular carburation: Ferrari claimed a power output of 380 bhp at a dizzying 10,000 rpm. The car's chassis was atypical, with a multi-tubular spaceframe stiffened by aluminium panels and a glassfibre undertray that housed the fuel tanks. The P4 weighed in at 1950 lb (885 kg); the works claimed a top speed of 198 mph (317 km/h), making it marginally slower than the 7-litre North American challenger. It was, however, lighter, more responsive and much easier on its brakes.

This became evident at the car's 1967 Daytona 24 Hours debut. Ford entered six cars, Ferrari two P4s backed up by two privateer P3/4s, also known as 412Ps (effectively P3s uprated to P4 specification but with 24-valve engines fed by Weber carburettors). The Ford GT40 MkIIs took a pummelling on the Florida track's challenging mix of banking and road circuit, and dropped like flies. P4s finished first and second, with a P3/4 rounding out the podium places. The sole remaining GT40 ended up seventh, seventy-three laps behind the winner. Enzo Ferrari had got his revenge.

The most beautiful racing car of all time? The P4 is certainly a candidate. A riot of compound curves, Ferrari hasn't built a prettier sports-prototype since.

This is a close physical reproduction of the classic P4, created for a Swiss enthusiast. The original was built to vanquish Ford in endurance racing. Although it never outdid its better-funded rival at Le Mans, it did score an emphatic victory at the 1967 Daytona 24 Hours, humbling the Detroit giant in the process.

The gorgeous Campagnolo wheels, with giant knock-off centre spinners, were once a Ferrari constant. Not even myriad vents and ducts blight the overall picture: this is as wondrous as racing cars get.

Left: The rear deck lifts up in one piece to reveal the V12 engine. The 36-valve, all-alloy unit fitted to the factory racers was derived from a Grand Prix item. Unusually, it was fuel-injected rather than carburreted.

Opposite: It's doubtful as to whether the P4 was ever very efficient aerodynamically, and it lacked the horsepower of many of its rivals. It was, however, a race winner and a landmark Ferrari.

1967 FERRARI 330GTC SPECIALE

By the late 1960s, Ferrari rarely strayed outside its catalogue models, having found that building one-off or small-series cars proved too much of a distraction. There were always exceptions, however. Should a customer be a close personal friend of Enzo Ferrari – or a monarch – then chances are something special could be rustled up. This dramatic coupé is a case in point. Commissioned by Princess Lilian de Rethy, whose husband, Leopold III of Belgium, had been a loyal patron since the firm's first hesitant steps towards greatness, just four of these machines were made. Ostensibly based on the production 330GTC, itself not lacking in exclusivity, such was the extensive reworking of the car's profile that the Speciale was considered a different model altogether.

Mechanically identical to the regular 330GTC (save for the fourth car, the V12 engine of which had a larger displacement), this model had a Pininfarina re-skin that resulted in a larger machine. The designers borrowed styling cues from the Tom Tjaarda-penned 365 California and 500 Superfast models, and the extended overhangs, larger glasshouse and Perspex-shrouded headlights lent it an entirely new look. The wrap-around rear screen was then especially novel, and was carried over to the Dino 206GT (see p. 218). Each car was entirely hand-built, and was tailored to suit the client, although all four were initially finished in a pale-blue metallic hue. The princess's car was displayed at the January 1967 Brussels Salon, and she retained it until her death in June 2002 at the age of 85, by which time it had covered fewer than 20,000 miles (32,200 km).

Distinct from the series, but closely related, was a one-off variation of the 330GTC built for Leopoldo Pirelli, boss of the tyre manufacturer. With a 4.4-litre V12 engine from the forthcoming 365, and riding on special 15-in. (381-mm) Campagnolo wheels, the 'Pirelli Speciale' was one of the fastest road-going Ferraris yet built. Another one-off 330GTC was created for Ferrari's North American concessionaire, Luigi Chinetti, its Zagato bodywork being irredeemably ugly.

It was never offered for general sale, so you had to be very well connected to land a Speciale. Princess Lilian de Rethy and her husband, King Leopold III of Belgium, the model's originators, had been loyal supporters of Enzo Ferrari since he first started making cars under his own name.

With shades of earlier Superfast models, this subspecies of the 330GTC featured a larger glasshouse, augmented overhangs, and buttresses that ran the full length of the rear deck. Predictably the work of Turin styling house Pininfarina, it was instigated at the behest of Belgian nobility and was never a catalogue model. More recently, the firm has built equally shadowy small-run cars for Middle Eastern royalty.

Opposite: The 330GTC's all-alloy V12 engine was left standard in this new application, and produced almost 300 bhp before performance-enhancement.

Below: The rear-three-quarter view highlights the massive rear overhang. The unusual buttresses mirror those found on the glorious Dino 'baby Ferrari'.

1967 'FERRARI' DINO 206GT/246GT

When is a Ferrari not a Ferrari? When it's a Dino. It seems unlikely decades after the fact, but when the achingly pretty 206GT was ushered in at the 1967 Turin Salon, the Ferrari cognoscenti was outraged. It had a V6 engine – in the middle – with a displacement of just 2 litres. It didn't even have a prancing horse badge. Fast-forward to the present and the Dino is deified for its timeless beauty and tenacious handling.

This was a product close to Enzo Ferrari's heart. His only (legitimate) son and heir, Alfredo – or Dino – had died of kidney failure at a tragically youthful twenty-four. The father was keen to honour his son's memory – and take the fight to German rival Porsche, with its 911. The Dino 'junior supercar' represented Ferrari's first link with the industrial giant Fiat, the conglomerate building Ferrari engines while also using them in its own blue-collar range-toppers; before the decade was over, Fiat would buy the majority shareholding in the firm.

Styled by the brilliant Leonardo Fioravanti, and bodied in aluminium by Scaglietti, the 206GT had a jewel-like all-alloy engine that was turned sideways and squeezed behind the occupants. Yet production lasted barely two years before the 246GT emerged at the 1969 Turin Salon. This model was marginally longer, taller and heavier (the body was now steel, the engine block cast iron); the enlarged 2418-cc V6 produced 195 bhp, so performance was sparkling: a top speed of 148 mph (238 km/h) and a 0–60 mph (0–96.5 km/h) time of a whisker under seven seconds. Joined in 1972 by the GTS edition – complete with removable roof panel – the Dino lasted until May 1974, when it was replaced (but not in spirit) by the altogether less memorable 308GT4. There should have been a national day of mourning.

Arguably the most beautiful mid-engined road car ever produced by Ferrari – and its first – the Dino was intended to act as a sister brand, with Porsche firmly in its sights.

ZH·94896

ZH · 94896

From all angles the Dino is simply an exquisite and masterful piece of packaging: photographs really don't provide a true sense of scale. This is a small car, one that punches well above its weight. The Prancing Horse badge in the front grille (opposite) was a non-factory addition.

Below: Sculptured air-intakes along the flanks were first seen on the Tom Tjaarda-penned Ferrari 365 California, and were transposed perfectly on to the Dino. The gracefully arced rear buttresses evoke memories of the many Pininfarina show cars of the 1950s.

Opposite: The compact V6 initially had a displacement of 2 litres, which was subsequently increased to 2.4 litres. It's one of the best-sounding, most vocal engines ever produced.

1968 FERRARI 365GTB/4/365GTS/4

It seems improbable now, but when it was unveiled at the 1968 Geneva Salon, there was palpable disappointment within the motoring media over Ferrari's new big-boned and full-bodied GT. And this was less to do with the car's appearance than with what it seemingly represented. Created in just one week by a sleep-deprived Leonardo Fioravanti, the Daytona coupé – or, to use its less romantic factory designation, the 365GTB/4 – was a masterpiece: seemingly all bonnet, with one perfect arc sweeping from a pointed nose to the cropped tail, the taut roofline curving ever so gently around the shallow side glazing. Nothing was allowed to interrupt the airflow, with wipers concealed beneath a lip at the base of the windscreen, and tiny door handles all but invisible at the top of the beltline.

Although viewed in some quarters as anachronistic when compared to some of its challengers, the 'Daytona', in period, was likely the quickest production car on the market. The open GTS/4 edition remains a work of automotive art – and one that's been cribbed ad infinitum.

Though capable of 174 mph (280 km/h) and 0–100 mph (0–161 km/h) in just 12.6 seconds, the Daytona initially suffered by comparison with the car its performance eclipsed: the Lamborghini Miura. The Sant'Agata upstart had created a machine for which the term 'supercar' was coined, placing the engine behind the driver – and transversely. When Ferrari announced its replacement for the 275GTB, many expected a mid-engined retort from Maranello, so the arrival of the Daytona effectively meant – if you follow the logic – that the Prancing Horse was playing it too safe. Except that the Miura was never altogether finished, and it showed: the Daytona was an infinitely better car.

Of the 1400 or so examples made up until 1975, those most coveted today are the Spiders. Just 125 of these convertibles were reputedly made by Scaglietti, with only seven in right-hand-drive. Considering the 100 per cent price premium over the coupé, it's no great surprise that many closed cars have gone under the knife, with replicas emerging.

Less than 10 per cent of all Daytonas were sold in the Spider configuration. The desirability of the model as it reached collector car status resulted in many coupés going under the knife and having their roofs removed to replicate the Spider's silhouette.

Considering its not inconsiderable
proportions and general heft,
it's a surprise that the Daytona
proved a useful competition tool,
taking overall victory in the European
GT championship, and class honours
at Le Mans.

Left: Competition-configured Daytonas were offered with varying specifications, with the V12 powerhouse kicking out north of 400 bhp in its ultimate state of tune.

Opposite: With the wider wheels necessitating flared wheelarches, and Perspex panels replacing heavier glass, the competition variation of the strain looked altogether more purposeful. The model was still racking up significant successes long after production had officially come to an end.

1969   PININFARINA SIGMA

'Competition improves the breed' was a common mantra in the 1960s. The trickledown effect of technology dreamed up in the motor-sport firmament supposedly resulted in better road cars for Everyman. The validity of this statement is debatable, not least when it comes to safety. This was a decade that witnessed seismic shifts in performance and methods of construction, but trackside deaths and serious injuries were commonplace. A blind eye was turned to reducing the likelihood of such catastrophes.

Although every inch the concept car, the Sigma wasn't an act of starry-eyed whimsy: it was designed to save lives.

The editors of Switzerland's influential *Automobil Revue* initiated the Sigma project as a means of showcasing ideas on how to build a safer racing car. Enlisting a cadre of such respected experts as Professor Ernst Fiala (later engineering chief of Volkswagen) and Dr Michael Henderson (an Australian physician and authority on race safety), the magazine's biggest coup was tapping Enzo Ferrari for the supply of a 1967 312 Grand Prix car to use as a basis for the project. Pininfarina would build the car, with Paolo Martin interpreting the ideas to create an attractive whole. The respected journalist and former Le Mans winner Paul Frére was on board to offer a driver's point of view.

Designing a car on the basis that an accident is highly likely, a rigid safety cell was created with crumple zones front and rear to absorb forces on impact. Pontoons were added to the car's flanks to dissipate some energy in the event of being hit side on, and a quick-release mechanism between the crash helmet and headrest was put in place to reduce the risk of neck injuries.

Many of the ideas promoted on the Sigma were never applied in motor sport, and others arrived in altered forms in the decades that followed. Ultimately, it was a safety crusade led by racing legend Jackie Stewart that brought about the painfully slow realization that drivers weren't expendable.

Created by a cabal of talented engineers and safety experts, and styled by Paolo Martin of Pininfarina, the Sigma ultimately didn't affect the face of motor sport. However, some features have since indirectly filtered down into racing-car architecture.

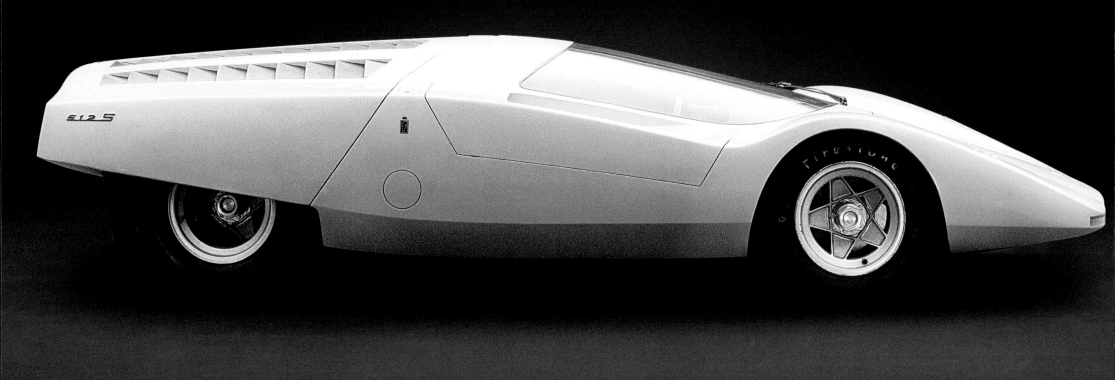

1969 FERRARI PININFARINA 512S BERLINETTA SPECIALE

Unquestionably one of the greatest concept cars of all time, Pininfarina's 1969 Turin Salon show-stopper was never a viable production model – not even close. But that wasn't the point. Hinting at the future was its purpose, even if little thought was given to the present. This wedge-shaped projectile married sports-prototype racing technology with radical styling flair, and if the purple gush of the press release was to be believed, it was built as 'an exploration of new aerodynamic solutions', with the close collaboration of engineers from the Polytechnic of Turin.

Underneath the dart-like outline lay a Ferrari 512S semi-monocoque frame with a 4993-cc V12 mounted amidships. The chassis itself once formed part of a 312P sports-prototype that had returned to Maranello after a fiery crash at Monza. It was subsequently used as a basis for developing the 512S racer, and, with an engine block from a 612 Can–Am (Canadian–American Challenge Cup) car, it was handed over to Pininfarina once the racing department had no more use for it.

The design aces didn't hold back. Aside from the wheelarches, there was scarcely a curve to the entire body. The front end, unencumbered by a radiator, ensured a low frontal area; the huge one-piece plastic windscreen swept almost horizontally to the rear engine deck, replete with three rows of lateral cooling louvres. To either side of the glasshouse were long rectangular slots to carry cooling air to the radiators, although onlookers with a technical bent doubted that this would ever work. Below the upswept rear skirt, the gearbox and four exhaust pipes poked out menacingly, Pininfarina deliberately not hiding the donor car's competition pedigree. At just 38⅝ in. (980 mm) from top to bottom, and almost twice as wide, the car's most extreme feature was the one-piece flip-up canopy in place of conventional doors. It required a certain amount of physical dexterity to get inside, but you looked good once there. With this starry-eyed slice of futurism, looking good was the important bit.

Despite this wonder-wedge being a pure concept car, several design features were watered down and used on production Ferraris, not least the slats atop the rear deck.

The lift-up rear end allowed easy access to the V12 engine mounted amidships. The one-piece front-hinged canopy was altogether less practical, entry and egress requiring a considerable degree of physical dexterity.

1970 FERRARI 512M 'SUNOCO'

On paper, it couldn't fail. Take one competitive racing car, add a stellar race team for which success always seemed preordained, and this uniquely American Ferrari racer should have been a winner. Instead, it's remembered more for what it didn't achieve.

Revered U.S. racing driver Mark Donohue called it 'the unfair advantage': a method of honing and perfecting a racing car to the point that it does most of the work for you. Rather than having to nurse a car and drive around problems, with one that was properly set up, you wouldn't have to. Together with team owner Roger Penske, Donohue perfected the art. Yet, for all their efforts, this 512M never won a single race.

They got an A for effort, though. The car started life as a 512S, Ferrari's retort of 1970 to the all-conquering Porsche 917. Driven in a handful of Can–Am races that year by Jim Adams, it was sold at season's end to Ferrari dealer Kirk White, who entrusted its preparation to Penske for 1971. The Philadelphia team stripped the car, making alterations to the suspension and steering geometry, while engine builder Traco prepared the pair of 5-litre V12 engines that came with the car.

Fitted with a new 512M (Modificato) body, and painted in Sunoco's corporate metallic blue and yellow, the Penske-Ferrari debuted in the 1971 Daytona 24 Hours, where Donohue and David Hobbs battled for the lead before an accident and electrical issues dropped them to an eventual third. Wearing a new ultra-light body made by Barry Plasti Glass for March's Sebring 12 Hours, it crashed its way down the order to sixth by the end of the race. Donohue retired it from June's Le Mans 24 Hours while running in second place, and a broken steering tie-rod saw him spear off the road at Watkins Glen. A Can–Am race at the same venue – on the same weekend – ended with a holed piston. A sad, if predictable, outcome.

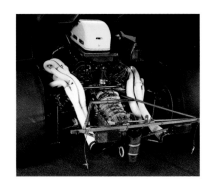

It looked fabulous, it was quick and it remains as charismatic as any inanimate object ever can be, yet the Penske-Ferrari failed to translate its considerable promise into race-winning success.

Opposite: The ultra-businesslike cockpit had all the important instruments in direct line of sight, with secondary switches sited to the driver's right together with the sill-mounted gearlever.

Below: The dramatic bodywork was a development of Ferrari's own 512M, but was created in the United States especially for the Penske squad. It was finished in the corporate livery of the team's sponsor, Sunoco.

The dart-like profile reflected the move in sports-prototypes away from curves towards more geometric shapes. Campaigned by a cadre of talented drivers, and with arguably the greatest race team North America has ever produced running the show, this machine would prove a rare – but glorious – failure.

1970 FERRARI PININFARINA MODULO

The reaction was one of shell-shocked bewilderment. As the covers were lifted off Pininfarina's latest concept car at the 1970 Geneva Salon, onlookers were left in no doubt: the legendary styling house had gone for broke. Chief designer Paolo Martin had produced an outline that pushed envelopes and broke moulds as to what was possible when designing a car. It helped that there was no intention of ever making more than the solitary prototype.

From nose to tail, the profile was one uninterrupted curved line, rising to the driver's seat before tapering off at the car's cropped tail. It had a flush-fitting, one-piece windscreen-cum-canopy, and twenty-four large holes in the rear deck to cool the quad-cam V12 engine, but the most radical feature was the full-width body wraps over the wheels. The Modulo was based on a 512S sports-racer chassis and running gear, and Pininfarina's flowery prose from the period talked of a top speed of a preposterous 223 mph (359 km/h). Most onlookers doubted if there was any steering lock, considering the close proximity of the bodywork to the front wheels.

Though the car was latterly lauded as a work of automotive art, the motoring media of the day were scathing about what was seen as a great folly. *Road & Track* commented: 'This is a real no-holds-barred formula libre styling effort, which produced some intriguing verbal reactions at first sight. "Gee", "gaw", "gosh", "holy mac", "dio", "ach", "blimey", "mon dieu" and "gottverdommer" were among the more recognisable and printable ones … . Many felt the designer had overreached himself.'

First shown in a striking black, red and white finish, with a horizontal split motif, by the time the car appeared at the Turin Salon later that year it had been repainted in its current white. For all the carping from the press, the Modulo was certainly a huge hit in the design community, earning Pininfarina twenty-two international awards. With such a rich back catalogue to choose from, this is among the select few cars retained in the firm's private collection.

Looking for all the world as though it had just escaped from a science-fiction movie, this bold styling exercise was a darling of the design community. In stark contrast, certain sections of the media positively *hated* it.

The knee-high profile was the work of Pininfarina's Paolo Martin; entry into the cabin was via the canopy, which moved forward. It's unlikely that the car was genuinely drivable above walking pace, but as a flight of automotive design fancy the Modulo has never been bettered.

1973   FERRARI 365BB/512BB

First shown in prototype form at the 1971 Turin Salon, the original 365BB eschewed contemporary styling gimmicks, instead drawing inspiration from the earlier Modulo (see p. 247) and 512S Berlinetta Speciale (see p. 237) show cars. Designed by Pininfarina's super-talented Leonardo Fioravanti, it was perhaps less dramatic than the Lamborghini Countach launched that same year. It had, however, a more cohesive silhouette, one that was unencumbered by the eye-watering plastic addenda that afflicted its Sant'Agata rival in future years.

Like the 512S, the 365BB had a dart-like outline, with a typically Ferrari tubular semi-monocoque chassis. In a break with tradition, power came from a new, mid-mounted, longitudinally sited Flat – or Boxer – V12 engine based in part on the 312B Grand Prix-car unit from 1969. Unfortunately, although the configuration of this engine had the advantage of a low centre of gravity – the crankshaft was about 20 in. (508 mm) off the deck – all benefit was negated by the fact that the transaxle sat under the engine, offset from the centreline. The net result was a tail-biased 40:60 weight distribution, making it a mite tricky to tame when pressed hard in corners.

However, Ferrari wasn't finished. In 1976 the 365 morphed into the 4929-cc 512BB, the extra displacement not correlating to extra horsepower, but there was a 10 per cent rise in torque. Yet by the time the Berlinetta Boxer made way for the Testarossa in 1984, it had lost its four Weber carburettors and 10 bhp to emission-friendly Bosch K-Jetronic fuel-injection, the BBi being more tractable but less urgent as a result. Ferrari's claim of a top speed of 180 mph (290 km/h) was at best optimistic, 160 mph (257 km/h) being more probable. Whatever the truth, it remains a classic old-school supercar and easily among the prettiest.

Ferrari's retort to Lamborghini's outré Countach was visually less dramatic but a much better all-round car.

Below: Styled by Pininfarina's Leonardo Fioravanti, the Berlinetta Boxer was achingly pretty in standard form. This example features non-factory spoilers and wider wheels.

Opposite: The lift-up rear deck afforded easy access to the Flat-12 engine. The gearbox that sat beneath the powerplant was slightly less accessible.

1975　FERRARI 308GTB/GTS

To anyone whose formative years were the early 1980s, this car has particular resonance. In one of the greatest acts of product placement ever perpetuated on the small screen, the 308GTS became the real star of the hugely popular detective show *Magnum, P.I.* Little wonder that these cars are still generically referred to as 'Magnum Ferraris'.

Introduced at the October 1975 Paris Salon, the overwhelmingly pretty 308GTB more than made amends for the lacklustre 308GT4 that had supposedly replaced the much-loved Dino 246 a year earlier. This was a more fitting substitute, its outline, penned by Leonardo Fioravanti, sharing some design cues with its 365BB big brother. With a 3-litre V8 designed by Franco Rocchi mounted amidships, the 308GTB was markedly different from previous Ferrari road cars in having a glassfibre body. Some 712 cars later, more conventional steel hulls became the norm. At the September 1977 Frankfurt Motor Show, the range was augmented by the even more desirable 308GTS: thanks to a removable roof panel that could be stowed behind the seats, it soon outsold its sibling by three to one. The introduction of fuel-injection from late 1980 appeased increasingly stringent U.S. emissions regulations, but with a corresponding drop off in performance. This was alleviated from late 1982 by the arrival of the 4-valve-per-cylinder Quattrovalvole edition that boosted power to a healthy 240 bhp.

Such was the commercial success of the 308 that it outlived its natural lifespan, morphing into the 328 in early 1985. With lightly revised styling and a technical makeover (the most obvious revision being the adoption of anti-lock brakes in its final year), it remained in production until 1989 before making way for the less pretty 348. Even now, the 308/328-series remains hugely popular with those looking to make the leap into first-time Ferrari ownership, with more than 15,000 of all types from which to choose.

Ferrari's 308-series vastly increased the company's penetration in several key markets, and led to a raft of brilliant V8 junior supercars, which flourish to this day.

Ferrari old-timers were initially hesitant in adopting a V8 model – Ferraris should have V12s, they railed – even though the *scuderia* had won two Formula One world titles using eight-cylinder engines. When the 308 (here in GTS configuration) finally broke cover in 1975, the doubters were soon silenced: it swiftly exceeded all sales expectations.

1987   FERRARI F40

Assembling a group of motoring journalists and asking them to agree on anything other than mutual enmity is near impossible – unless the question is 'What is your favourite supercar?' Not best, but favourite. It's a subtle but important distinction, for while the F40 has its flaws, anyone who has ever attempted to tame it has come away enamoured. It is simply the most exhilarating road car imaginable, and its place in Ferrari lore is assured, being the last example of the marque to be signed off personally by Enzo himself.

The most fun, most boisterous supercar ever? Without doubt, it has to be the F40. What it lacked in elegance, it more than made up for in performance, being the first off-the-peg 200-mph (320-km/h) production car.

Derived from the 288GTO Evoluzione conceived for the ultimately aborted Group B racing category, this remarkable machine was built to take the fight to Porsche's advanced 959 and be finished in time for the marque's fortieth anniversary in 1987. The F40 was intended from the outset as a no-frills racing car for the road: 400 would be made, and they would all be red.

Powering the car was a 2936-cc variation of the GTO's twin-turbocharged V8, developing 471 bhp. The dramatic body was styled by Leonardo Fioravanti of Pininfarina; the body panels were made of carbon-fibre, Kevlar and aluminium; and, thanks to its small frontal area and attention to reducing drag, it had a coefficient of 0.34 cd. Top speed was an honest 202 mph (325 km/h), making it the first genuine production car to exceed the double ton.

Launched just as a supercar boom saw residual prices of Ferraris skyrocket, what was intended strictly as a limited edition became a regular production model: by the end, in 1992, some 1315 had found homes. More remarkable still was the car's ability to take the fight to McLaren's mighty F1 in BPR GT racing in the mid-1990s. Although long out of production, and despite being technically obsolete, it recorded one win per season from 1994 to 1996.

Below: Styled by the once omnipresent Leonardo Fioravanti, and honed in a wind tunnel, the F40 was conceived as a road-going racing car. Although there was nowhere for it to race when new, the model took the fight to the McLaren F1 in BPR GT racing in the mid-1990s.

Opposite: The huge rear wing isn't there for purely aesthetic reasons: it affords genuine downforce. And the F40 needs it, too. This twin-turbo, V8-equipped monster has no driver aids, no ABS or traction control. It's down to pilot ability to get the best out of the machine.

1989 FERRARI 348

Though never held in the wider public's affections in the same way as its 308/328 predecessor, the 348 was a commercially successful model that helped Ferrari weather the global recession of the early 1990s – the same recession that claimed several challengers. Announced at the 1989 Frankfurt Motor Show, it represented a major departure from preceding Maranello supercars in being homologated worldwide rather than differing in detail between different markets. By 1995 more than 9000 had been sold.

Distinct from earlier V8 Ferraris, the 348 did away with the usual tubular-steel chassis; in its place was a pressed-steel item with a tubular engine subframe. It also had its 3.4-litre Tipo F119D unit sited longitudinally rather than transversely for a truly competition-inspired layout (much like its F40 big brother). The engine was a development of the enduring powerplant designed by Franco Rocchi for the outgoing 328. Power output was increased to 300 bhp at an eye-watering 7200 rpm; the gearbox was mounted on to the rear of the engine. Ferrari claimed a top speed of 165 mph (266 km/h), with the 0–60 mph (0–96.5 km/h) sprint taking a mere 5.5 seconds.

Clearly inspired by the Testarossa, not least in its slatted side vents, the 348's outline was, predictably, the work of Pininfarina. Bodied in steel except for the aluminium bonnet and boot (with glassfibre being used for the front and rear bumpers), build quality was also markedly improved over previous models. Offered in closed form ('TB', for 'transverse berlinetta') or with a lift-out roof panel ('TS', for 'transverse targa'), both models were replaced by the GTB and GTS versions respectively from late 1993. These boasted an extra 20 bhp and styling revisions in line with such sister models as the 512TR (itself a development of the Testarossa). Rarest of all was the Zagato-customized Elaborazione edition. Just twelve of the envisaged twenty cars were made, with styling revisions that teetered on the edge of vulgarity.

Oddly marginalized while it awaits classic status, the 348 was nonetheless a significant sales success for Ferrari, and one that saw the marque return to the Le Mans 24 Hours in 1993, more than a decade after its last appearance.

Although perhaps not the prettiest of
Ferraris, the 348 was certainly dramatic,
if quick to date. The side strakes and
rear louvres mimicked those of its
Testarossa/512TR big brother.

1995 FERRARI F50

Sandwiched between the F40 and the Enzo, this remarkable machine has always suffered by comparison. This is less because of the way it drives – it is truly, really brilliant – and more to do with the way it looks. Unconventionally attractive to some and conventionally unattractive to others, the F50 polarized opinion from the moment it was unveiled at the 1995 Geneva Salon. Here was a car designed with aerodynamic efficiency paramount, a 202-mph (325-km/h) blunt instrument created to re-establish Ferrari's bragging rights. After the F40 ended production in 1992, the marque had been without a talisman, Jaguar stealing the limelight with the 217-mph (349-km/h) XJ220 and McLaren with its extraordinary F1. Ferrari had to come back fighting.

The F50 was powered by a normally aspirated 4.7-litre V12 Tipo F130 engine derived – if only in part – from the 1991 642 Grand Prix challenger. Formula One technology was also apparent in the monocoque, which was manufactured entirely of carbon-fibre, the engine acting as an integral load-bearing structure. Distinct from its rivals, the F50 featured a removable roof panel that allowed owners to convert the car to alfresco form in a matter of seconds. Honed and tweaked in Pininfarina's wind tunnel, the outré rear aerofoil was there for more than just show, providing downforce to keep the rear end planted. Huge engine scoops were hollowed out of the car's flanks, and the engine was visible through a transparent cover. Inside, racer-inspired reference points were all too obvious: while the thickly bolstered seats were trimmed in leather, the combined digital and analogue instrument binnacle and acres of unpainted carbon-fibre were clearly nods to the firm's competition programme.

Sadly there would be no serious motor-sport campaign with the F50. Plans to race the model in the burgeoning BPR GT series came to naught after three racing versions had been built: the plug was pulled at the eleventh hour. In total just 349 F50s were made, one fewer than Ferrari believed it could sell.

The nearest thing to a road-going Formula One car? Hardly, but the F50 was cutting-edge stuff in the mid-1990s. Its fabulous V12 engine used technology borrowed from the Maranello firm's Grand Prix squad.

Left: If there was one criticism routinely levelled at the F50 in period, it was that it wasn't entirely pretty. But in a car capable of such extreme levels of performance, aerodynamic considerations come into play: here, form really does follow function. This remains a phenomenal car to drive, at any speed.

Opposite: A transparent cover allowed spectators a view of the race-bred V12 engine, while the ability to remove the roof provided that bleeding-scalp sensation as one aimed for the 200-mph (320-km/h) barrier.

2002 FERRARI ENZO

Ushering in an era in which Pininfarina and Ferrari set about pushing envelopes and breaking moulds, the arrival of the Enzo at the 2002 Paris Salon was met with predictably dumbstruck bewilderment. Was it meant to look like that? This radical, geometric device wasn't beautiful – not even close – but this was perhaps the most advanced road car of the modern age, a car for which purity of line clearly took a backseat to packaging and aerodynamic requirements. And besides, all 399 units had been pre-sold at nearly £500,000 a pop.

Unusually for a supercar, the outline here was influenced more by aerodynamics and packaging requirements than by artistic abstraction. The design borrowed heavily from Formula One experience, the most obvious Grand Prix-inspired feature being the raised nose, flanked by a pair of radiators sited ahead of each front wheel. Hot air was directed through ducts to the outer body so as to prevent under-body airflow from upsetting the car's balance. The Enzo's structure comprised a carbon-fibre monocoque on to which the roof was then bonded. Power came from a 650-bhp, 6-litre V12 engine mounted on a cast alloy subframe, with push-rod double wishbone suspension front and rear. Weighing in at just 3009 lb (1365 kg), it was slightly heavier than Ferrari's technicians had envisaged, but this extraordinary machine could still sprint to 60 mph (96.5 km/h) in just 3.5 seconds; to 125 mph (201 km/h) in 9.5 seconds; and on to 217 mph (349 km/h) overall.

Notwithstanding the leather-clad Sparco seats and door inserts, the car's cabin was stark, mainly bare carbon-fibre. There were no token concessions to luxury: no air-conditioning, not even a radio. The steering wheel incorporated multiple function settings governing suspension set-ups and throttle responses, while four-point harnesses came as standard. Perhaps this was just as well: the Enzo could lap Ferrari's Fiorano test track a scarcely believable 4.5 seconds faster than the previous F50 supercar. It also found competition success of a sort, providing the platform for the Maserati MC12 that upset the rule-makers in GT racing – despite the fact that the Enzo road car was actually faster!

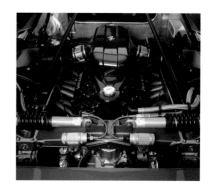

Stealth Bomber meets supercar? The Enzo polarized opinion like few other cars when unleashed in 2002. It set the template for more 'challenging' Ferraris, where flaunting technology was as important as aesthetic considerations. Its V12 engine acted as a structural member and produced a whopping 650 bhp.

Below: Although far from pretty, few cars possess as much presence as an Enzo. Conceived as a road car, it nevertheless went on to a lead a secondary existence as a racing car, sharing most of its DNA with the Maserati MC12.

Opposite: Formula One technology coursed through the Enzo. The steering wheel housed controls for traction control, wing angles, suspension-setting and umpteen other functions; its upper rim incorporated five LED lights that illuminated in increments of 500 rpm as one passed the 5500 rpm mark.

Opposite: Aside from the leather-clad, Sparco-made bucket seats and door cards, the Enzo's cabin was awash with acres of unpainted carbon-fibre. There were no concessions to civility: no electric windows, stereo or other accoutrement found in even the most basic of hatchbacks.

Right: Aerodynamically advanced, and able to lap Ferrari's Fiorano test track only a few seconds shy of recently obsolete Grand Prix cars, the Enzo was the first truly landmark supercar of the new millennium.

THE NAMES BEHIND THE LEGENDS

DESIGNERS

LEONARDO FIORAVANTI
b.1938

A supremely gifted designer responsible for styling eight landmark Ferraris (the Daytona, 365BB and 308GTB among them), this super-enthusiastic craftsman has yet to receive wider recognition. This is due, in part, to Pininfarina's policy of not attributing credit to individual employees. Born in Milan, Fioravanti trained as an engineer before joining the Turin styling house in 1964; eight years later he was the firm's director of research. He would remain there until the mid-1980s before brief spells at Ferrari and Alfa Romeo. Together with his sons Luca and Matteo, he formed an automotive design and architectural design consultancy, Fioravanti srl, in 1987. Eleven years later he created a Ferrari-based concept car dubbed the C100 to celebrate Enzo Ferrari's centenary.

MAURO FORGHIERI
b.1935

One of the great engine designers of the post-war era, this Modena-born engineer obtained a degree in mechanical engineering from the University of Bologna, initially with a view to working in aviation. After being introduced to Enzo Ferrari by his father, he became part of the racing team in 1962 and was thrust into the role of chief engineer aged just twenty-seven. He conceived the 312-series of cars, and is famed for his Flat-12 engines that helped power Niki Lauda and Jody Scheckter to Formula One titles. Forghieri left Ferrari in 1987 to join Lamborghini Engineering, then under Chrysler control. He was commissioned to design the new V12 engine that was used by the Larrousse Grand Prix squad during the 1989 season. After joining the reborn Bugatti in 1992, Forghieri worked on the EB110 supercar project before forming his own Oral Engineering consultancy two years later.

VITTORIO JANO
1891–1965

Milan-born Jano's contribution to the evolution of the racing car is immense, and he is justifiably a legend in motor-sport history. After beginning his career at Fiat in 1911, he moved to Alfa Romeo eleven years later; there he created the P2 single-seater and the 6C-series of sports and racing cars that won the Targa Florio and Mille Miglia under Scuderia Ferrari. He left for Lancia in 1937 and lent his genius to numerous projects, including the D50 Grand Prix car. After Lancia pulled out of racing in 1955, Ferrari adopted the D50 design and Jano headed for Maranello along with it. He would remain with Ferrari until 1965, during which time he co-created the V6 Dino engine. After the death of his son, Giorgio, Jano tragically took his own life.

AURELIO LAMPREDI
1917–1989

Although Lampredi will be forever synonymous with Ferrari's early V12s, his career encompassed much, much more. The Livorno-born engineer began his career with Piaggio before moving to Isotta-Fraschini and then Reggiane, where he designed aircraft engines. Lampredi arrived at the nascent Ferrari in 1946 and proceeded to design a large, 4.5-litre V12 engine. A brief return to Isotta-Fraschini aside, he would remain with the firm and oversee Ferrari's racing efforts during the highly successful 1952 and 1953 seasons. Lampredi left the Maranello marque in 1955 after Ferrari assumed control of Lancia's racing team. In September of that year he joined Fiat as director of engine development, a position he would hold until 1977. He also worked with the Turin giant's Abarth competition department from 1973 to 1982.

GIOVANNI MICHELOTTI
1921–1980

A great – though unsung – star of car design, the prolific Michelotti was a pen for hire who would often juggle dozens of projects for rival manufacturers. He began his career at Stabilimenti Farina in 1936 and, after opening a small studio in his native Turin in 1949, offered his services to coachbuilders large and small – often without credit. If nothing else, his collaborations with Alfredo Vignale resulted in some of the most beautiful Ferraris of the 1950s. Under his own name, Michelotti created a number of one-off and small-series Ferraris for the firm's North American concessionaire, Luigi Chinetti. During the 1970s, Michelotti designed and built several Ferrari-based cars for Swiss dealer Willy Felber, one of which was subsequently adopted by British firm Panther Westwinds.

SERGIO SCAGLIETTI
b.1920

A largely unheralded star in Ferrari lore, Scaglietti entered the motor industry aged just thirteen, following the death of his father. He started out repairing and reworking existing cars before becoming a fully fledged coachbuilder. Like many of his contemporaries, Scaglietti worked more by eye and instinctive feel than from blueprints. In the 1950s, his eponymous *carrozzeria* rose to become the official body-builder to Ferrari, often translating Pinin Farina designs into production reality, as well as clothing the *scuderia*'s racing cars. A great friend of Enzo Ferrari, he too grew weary of Italy's constant political ructions during the 1960s, and similarly sold out to Fiat at the end of the decade. In 2004 Ferrari honoured his contribution to the firm's history with the launch of the range-topping 612 Scaglietti.

TOM TJAARDA
b.1934

Originally trained as an architect, Stevens Thompson Tjaarda van Starkenberg ultimately chose to follow his Dutch-born father, John, into car design. On graduation from the University of Michigan in 1958, he arrived in Italy and took up a position with Ghia in Turin. He planned to stay for six months, but has spent most of his career in Italy. During the mid-1960s Tjaarda joined Pininfarina, where he styled the strong-selling 330GT 2+2 and the sublime 365 California Spider. He subsequently returned to Ghia as chief designer, latterly under Ford ownership, before setting up his own consultancy. With more than seventy major projects under his belt, from the De Tomaso Pantera to the Ford Fiesta, his place in the car-design firmament is assured.

DRIVERS

GIANCARLO BAGHETTI
1934–1995

Although he never really capitalized on his early form, Baghetti nonetheless earned a distinguished place in Formula One history: after winning Grands Prix at Naples and Syracuse, he drove his Ferrari 156 to his third straight win in the 1961 French Grand Prix at Reims, which was part of the Formula One World Championship. It was the Italian's maiden series-level Grand Prix and marked the first time that any driver had won it on his debut. Unfortunately, Ferrari's fortunes dipped in 1962, and Baghetti's move to ATS a year on proved a disaster. After a one-off outing for Lotus in the 1967 Italian Grand Prix, Baghetti never drove in a Grand Prix again. A year later he retired from motor sport and went on to earn some measure of fame as a photographer. He died of cancer in 1995.

JUAN MANUEL FANGIO
1911–1995

A late starter in front-line motor racing, this Argentinian was an undoubted colossus of the sport during the 1950s. He was born of humble stock: his Italian émigré father was variously a plasterer and a potato farmer, young Juan finding work in a garage at ten years of age. Barely out of his teens, he began to build up a formidable reputation in South America for his efforts in gruelling cross-country races: in 1949 he won the 6000-mile (9656-km) Gran Premio Nacionale del Norte, a race from Buenos Aires to Lima and back. After an exploratory mission to Europe a year earlier, Fangio gained backing from the Argentine government to compete at Grand Prix level; he took his first win at Monaco in 1950 for Alfa Romeo. He subsequently moved from team to team, arriving at Ferrari in 1956 (replacing Alberto Ascari), where he took his fourth title, before leaving for Maserati, where he claimed his fifth and final World Championship crown.

DR GIUSEPPE FARINA
1906–1966

Destined to win the first-ever Formula One World Championship in 1950, 'Nino' Farina began his racing career in 1932, crashing heavily in the Aosta–Grand St Bernard hillclimb. Within ten years, the stylish Milanese had yet more accidents interspersed with major wins, primarily with Maseratis, before the Second World War intervened. In 1948 he won the Monaco Grand Prix, and occasionally drove for Ferrari in 1949. After taking his title for Alfa Romeo, the often ruthless Dottore (of engineering) was runner-up a year on, only for the marque to pull out of racing. Joining Ferrari full-time in 1952, Farina won the following year's German Grand Prix (his final Formula One win), but an accident at Monza in 1954 ultimately curtailed his career. After mounting a half-hearted attempt to race in the Indianapolis 500 in 1956 and 1957, he quit racing for good. He died in a car accident, on his way to watch the French Grand Prix, just short of his sixtieth birthday.

MIKE HAWTHORN
1929–1959

An underrated driver for all his achievements, this Yorkshire-born, Sussex-educated ace made his Formula One debut in the 1952 Belgian Grand Prix: he was fourth in a Cooper-Bristol. The blond Brit soon caught the attention of Enzo Ferrari, who offered him a drive for the following year. Hawthorn responded with a win in the 1953 French Grand Prix. After a two-year stint with Ferrari, he joined Vanwall (and then BRM) and, in 1955, triumphed in the Le Mans 24 Hours. There would be no joy, however, as he was involved in an accident with Pierre Levegh that claimed the lives of eighty-two spectators. Still on good terms with Enzo Ferrari – he briefly revisited Ferrari in 1955 during a scrappy season – Hawthorn returned full-time in 1957, and a year later was crowned Formula One drivers' champion. He then retired from racing, only to die the following January in a road accident.

PHIL HILL
b.1927

Despite winning the 1961 Formula One drivers' title for Ferrari, in addition to three wins in the Le Mans 24 Hours, this uncommonly cerebral driver remains criminally underrated. Brought up in Santa Monica, California, Hill started racing in the late 1940s with an MG TC. After success with larger cars, he attracted the attention of Ferrari's North American concessionaire, Luigi Chinetti, who picked him to drive for his NART (North American Racing Team) équipe. Chinetti advised Enzo Ferrari to offer the Californian a Le Mans drive for 1956, and the die was cast. Unfortunately, Hill was never able to capitalize on his Formula One title. Ferrari was eclipsed during the 1962 season, and Hill made a disastrous move to ATS for 1963. He was subsequently reduced to tooling around for the ailing Cooper and second-string Centro Sud BRM teams. He retired from front-line motor sport in 1967.

NIKI LAUDA
b.1949

This deep-thinking Viennese is a legend for much more than his driving. Lauda arrived at Ferrari in 1974, having shown sporadic flashes of form with the British March and BRM teams. He immediately proved a motivational force for a *scuderia* in the doldrums: he was World Champion in 1975 and again in 1977, and would likely have won the 1976 crown had he not suffered horrific burns after a crash at that year's German Grand Prix. Despite receiving the last rites, he rallied and was competing in the Italian Grand Prix barely eight weeks later. After moving to Brabham for 1978, he retired part way through the following season, only to make a comeback in 1982. He won the 1984 Formula One world title by half a point before walking away for good in 1985.

GIANCLAUDIO 'CLAY' REGAZZONI
1939–2006

The Swiss star Clay Regazzoni was tough, uncompromising, hugely brave and very popular with the fans, but his career was nonetheless blighted by controversy. Making his way through the junior formulae, he was implicated in the fatal crash that claimed the life of Chris Lambert during the European Formula Two race at Zandvoort in 1968. On joining Ferrari in Formula One in 1970, he won fourth time

out at Monza and was seen as a likely future champion. After sporadic results, he joined BRM in 1973, only to return to Ferrari a year on. He won the 1974 Monza Grand Prix and, two years later, the Long Beach Grand Prix. Dropped at the end of the season, he moved from Ensign to Shadow and then Williams, scoring an emotional win in the 1979 British round of the Formula One series. In 1980 he was back at Ensign, but was paralysed after a crash at Long Beach.

MICHAEL SCHUMACHER
b.1969

Arguably the greatest racing driver of all time, if only statistically, this controversial German was responsible for transforming Ferrari from pit-lane joke to unbeatable juggernaut during his tenure. Having shown impressive form in junior formulae, and with Mercedes-Benz in Group C sports cars, Schumacher made his Formula One debut at Spa in 1991 with the Jordan team. He was immediately poached by Benetton, for which he took back-to-back Formula One drivers' titles in 1994 and 1995, taking his first crown after biffing rival Damon Hill off the track in the final round. He joined Ferrari in 1996 when the *scuderia* was at a low ebb and built up the team around him. He took five consecutive championship wins from 2000 to 2004. In total, Schumacher started 250 Grands Prix and won an astounding ninety-one of them, also taking sixty-eight pole positions and seventy-six fastest laps.

JOHN SURTEES
b. 1934

Famously the only man to ever win the World Championship on two and four wheels, Surtees showed instant star quality with occasional drives for Lotus in 1960: he was second in the British Grand Prix, and captured pole position for the Portuguese Grand Prix. In 1963 he signed for Ferrari and took his first World Championship Formula One win in Germany that year, and the drivers' title in 1964. More championships should have followed, but the dogmatic Surtees and Machiavellian team manager, Eugenio Dragoni, didn't get along, and the Surrey-born star stormed out early in 1966. He immediately won the Mexican Grand Prix in a Maserati-powered Cooper before joining Honda, where he triumphed in the 1967 Italian Grand Prix. After a lacklustre spell with BRM, Surtees formed his own team, the Surtees Racing Organisation, which found success in Formula Two and Formula 5000 but failed to shine in Formula One.

GILLES VILLENEUVE
1950–1982

He won only six Grands Prix and polarized opinion among rivals and race fans alike: he was either the bravest driver who ever lived – or a lunatic. History views him as an icon of the sport, and rightfully so. This Quebec-born superstar began his motor-sport career racing snowmobiles before turning to four wheels. After proving himself in Formula Ford and Formula Atlantic, he made his Formula One debut driving for McLaren in the 1977 British Grand Prix. Joining Ferrari for the following season, he stayed with the *scuderia* until his death during qualifying for the 1982 Belgian Grand Prix, when his car collided with Jochen Mass's RAM March. His drive to second place in the 1979 French Grand Prix, during which he banged wheels with René Arnoux until the flag fell, is still routinely held up as one of the greatest on-track battles of all time.

GLOSSARY OF MOTORING TERMS AND STYLES

Axle
Shaft carrying the wheels and supporting the body via the road springs. Also refers to non-shaft wheel pairings transversely across the car in independent suspension.

Cam
Eccentric projection, usually elliptical in shape, on a shaft; it moves another component as the shaft revolves.

Camshaft
Shaft that revolves within a housing, often incorporating a number of cams, usually to operate valve gear. Can be driven by gears, chains or belts.

Carburettor
Mechanism that mixes petrol with air to atomize it and delivers this mixture to the engine inlet valves. It automatically adjusts mixture to suit the engine, road speed and atmospheric conditions.

Coil springs
Suspension mechanism of sprung-steel wire coiled into a helix.

Cubic capacity
Measurement of the total volume of an engine's cylinders swept by each piston in its bore. Engine capacity is measured in cubic centimetres (cc) or litres, 1000 cc being 1 litre; or in cubic inches, 1 cu. in. being 16.39 cc.

Garagiste
Derogatory term formerly used by the Italian and French motor-racing fraternity to describe constructors of humble origin, particularly such British firms as Cooper and Lotus.

Independent suspension
Method of attaching a vehicle's wheels so that each has its own independent linkage to the chassis or body. Each wheel is sprung independently so that it can move without affecting any other.

Ladderframe chassis
Chassis in which two spars are laid longitudinally and connected transversely by strengthening and support webs.

Leaf springs
Flat tempered steel joined together to form an elliptical shape in order to provide a springing effect between the axles and the car's chassis or body.

Live rear axle
Transverse beam axle connecting both road wheels and housing the differential and final drive.

Monocoque
Single-skin car body lacking longitudinal members.

Overhead camshaft
Camshaft(s) mounted above the cylinder head, at the opposite end of the crankshaft.

Panhard rod
An axle's lateral location device, situated between the car's body or chassis on one side, and an axle on the other.

Piston
A cylindrical component with one end closed and the other open, sealed into the engine cylinder with piston rings. Driven down the cylinder bore by the exploding fuel mixture, it bears on the connecting rods, which force the crankshaft to twist.

Privateer
An owner-driver not associated with a factory team.

rpm
Revolution per minute. Any measure of rotational speed. Usually refers to a crankshaft, but can also refer to road wheels.

Running gear
Components that underpin a car, in particular the engine, suspension and axles.

Semi-elliptic springs
A flat sprung-steel plate, or plates riveted together, forming a semi-ellipse in which the ends are joined to the body or chassis and the centre is joined to the axle. Semi-elliptical springs can be used in pairs as part of a live axle installation, or to create an independent suspension by fastening the spring transversely across the car, attaching it to the chassis in the centre and to the suspension at either end. In elliptical springs, one part is joined to the body and one to the axle. Quarter elliptics are only a quarter of an ellipse.

Spaceframe
A lightweight rigid framework made from chassis tubes in a geometric pattern to carry all the car's systems and provide a structure on which to hang the bodywork.

Supercharger
Mechanical air compressor used to charge an engine's cylinders with a greater quantity of petrol-and-air mixture than that inducted naturally.

Torsion bar
A sprung-steel bar used as a suspension mechanism in some applications by fastening the bar at one end and connecting it to a lever at the other.

Transaxle
A combined gearbox and final-drive unit positioned at the centreline of a drive axle and used to improve the car's balance or to save space through its compactness.

Turbocharger
A supercharger powered by the energy in the exhaust gases to compress the inlet charge.

Twin-cam
Term that describes the positioning of more than one camshaft, usually in a cylinder head, so that each camshaft operates directly above the valve it opens. This arrangement allows the engine designer to place the valves in the cylinder head at an optimal angle for the best gas flow, so increasing the engine's volumetric efficiency.

Wheelbase
Distance between the longitudinal centrelines of a vehicle's axles.

Wishbone
Pivoted, triangular links that connect a car's body or chassis to each wheel to form an independent suspension system.

DIRECTORY OF MUSEUMS
AND COLLECTIONS

FRANCE

Le Manoir de l'Automobile
4 rue de la Cour Neuve
35550 Lohéac
Tel: +33 (0)2 99 34 02 32
manoir-automobile.fr

GERMANY

Auto & Technik Museum Sinsheim
Museumsplatz
74889 Sinsheim
Tel: +49 (0)7261 9299 0
technik-museum.de

ITALY

Galleria Ferrari
Via Dino Ferrari 43
41053 Maranello
Modena
Tel: +39 (0)536 943204
galleria.ferrari.com

Museo dell'Automobile 'Carlo
Biscaretti di Ruffia'
Corso Unità d'Italia 40
10126 Turin
Tel: +39 (0)11 677666
museoauto.it

THE NETHERLANDS

Het Amsterdams Automuseum
Zwanenburgerdijk 281
1161 NL Zwanenburg
Tel: +31 (0)20 497 7291
amsterdams-automuseum.nl

UNITED KINGDOM

Donington Grand Prix Collection
Donington Park
Castle Donington
Derby
Derbyshire DE74 2RP
Tel: +44 (0)1332 811027
donington-park.co.uk/gpcollection

Haynes International Motor Museum
Sparkford
Yeovil
Somerset BA22 7LH
Tel: +44 (0)1963 440804
haynesmotormuseum.com

National Motor Museum
John Montagu Building
Beaulieu
Brockenhurst
Hampshire SO42 7ZN
Tel: +44 (0)1590 612345
beaulieu.co.uk

UNITED STATES

Blackhawk Museum
3700 Blackhawk Plaza Circle
Danville, CA 94506
Tel: +1 925 736 2277
blackhawkmuseum.org

Petersen Automotive Museum
6060 Wilshire Boulevard (at Fairfax)
Los Angeles, CA 90036
Tel: +1 323 930 2277
petersen.org

INDEX

*Main entries for cars, designers and drivers are shown in **bold**.*

A

Adams, Jim 240
Agnelli, Gianni 22, 23, 90, 93, 96
Al Faisal, Prince Mohamed 138
Alfa Romeo 9, 10, 11, 12, 13, 15
Ali Khan, Prince 138
Arnoux, René 282
Ascari, Alberto 13, 85, 280
ATS (Automobili Turismo e Sport) 18, 19
Auto Avio Costruzioni 12, 31
    Tipo 815 sports car 12–13, 31
Auto Italiano Sport 187
Autocar, The 13, 39
Automobil Revue 233
Autosport 16

B

Baghetti, Giancarlo 18, **280**
Baker, Jerry 127
Baracca, Count Enrico 9
Baracca, Francesco 9
Baracca, Countess Paolina 9
Barnard, John 25
Batchelor, Dean 173
Benetton 27
Bertone 15
Besana, Gabriele 31
Bizzarrini, Giotto 17, 18, 178
Boano, Mario 138
Bolster, John 16
Borgeson, Griff 18–19
Brabham, Jack 15, 142
Bracco, Giovanni 52
Bravarone, Aldo 194, 199
Brawn, Ross 27
Broadley, Eric 20
Byrne, Rory 27

C

Caniato, Alfredo and Augusto 11
Castellotti, Eugenio 127
Chinetti, Luigi 90, 99, 149, 213, 279, 281
Chiti, Carlo 17, 18
Coburn, James 194
Collins, Peter 138, 142
Colombo, Gioacchino 13, 31

Cooper 15
Cortese, Franco 13, 31
Costruzioni Meccaniche Nazionale 8
Courage, Piers 194

D

Delon, Alain 194
Donohue, Mark 240
Drogo, Piero 204
Duncan, Dale 68

E

Exner, Virgil 103

F

Fangio, Juan Manuel 14, 127, **280**
Farina, Battista 'Pinin' 16, 138
    see also Pinin Farina/ Pininfarina
Farina, Dr Giuseppe 68, **280**
Felber, Willy 279
Ferrari
    166 Spider Corsa 13, **30–37**
    212 Export 16, **38–45**

250 Europa 16, **60–67**, 90
250GT 16, 18–19
250GT Berlinetta 'Tour de France' 52, **132–37**
250GT California **148–53**
250GT Europa Berlinetta Speciale **106–13**
250GT Series 1 Cabriolet **138–41**
250GT SWB 52, 133, **154–61**, 178
250GTE **168–71**
250GTO 52, **178–85**
250GTZ Berlinetta **120–25**
250 Lusso 115, **186–93**
250MM 16, **52–59**, 133
250 Testa Rossa 74, **142–47**
275GTB **194–203**
288GTO 25
308GT4 218, 254
308GTB/GTS 25, **254–57**
330 America 169
330GTC Speciale **212–17**
330P4 **204–11**
342 America 16, 17, **46–51**

348 **262–65**
365BB/512BB **250–53**
365GTB/4/365GTS/4 22, **224–31**
375 America 'Agnelli' 16, **90–97**, 106
375 America Ghia **98–105**
375MM Berlinetta **114–19**
375MM Pinin Farina Spider **68–73**
375MM 'Rossellini' **74–77**
400 Superamerica Cabriolet **162–67**
400 Superamerica 'Coupé Aerodynamica' **172–77**
456GT 26
500 Mondial **84–89**
512M 'Sunoco' **240–45**
599GTB Fiorano 27
750 Monza **79–83**
860 Monza **126–31**
Daytona coupé *see* 365GTB/4/365GTS/4
Dino 206GT/246GT 106, 213, **218–23**
Dino V6 engine 14, 22
Enzo **270–77**

F40 **258–61**
F50 **266–69**, 270
F430 27
GTO 52
Pinin Farina Berlinetta
  coupé 52
Pininfarina 512S Berlinetta
  Speciale **236–39**
Pininfarina Modulo
  246–49
Pininfarina Sigma
  232–35
'Sharknose' 156 17
Testarossa 24, 25, 262
Type 125 13
Ferrari, Adalgisa 8
Ferrari, Alfredo 8
Ferrari, Alfredo, Jr 8
Ferrari, Alfredo 'Dino' 14, 85,
  87, 218
Ferrari, Enzo 7–22, 25, 39, 61,
  79, 90, 169, 218, 259
Ferrari, Laura 14, 18
Fiala, Ernst 233
Fiat 8, 12, 14, 22, 27, 173, 218
Fioravanti, Leonardo 218, 224,
  250, 254, 259, **278**
Florence, Lew 127

Ford, Henry II 20
Ford Motor Company
  19–20
  DFV (Double Four-Valve) V8
  20
  GT40 20
  GT40 MkII 204
Forghieri, Mauro 19, 22, **278**
Frère, Paul 233

G
Galluzzi, Vladimiro 120
Gardini, Girolamo 17–18
Gendebien, Olivier 142
Ghia 15, 99, 103, 105
Ginther, Richie 127
Giuliano, Luigi 52
Gobbato, Ugo 12
Gregory, Masten 68, 70, 72,
  79, 81, 83

H
Harrah, Bill 173
Hawthorn, Mike 79,
  280–81
Henderson, Dr Michael
  233
Hill, Phil 17, 18, 127, 142, **281**

Hobbs, David 240

I
Iacocca, Lee 19, 20
Ickx, Jackie 22

J
Jaguar
  E-type 162
  XJ220 267
Jano, Vittorio 14, **278**

K
Katskee, Loyal 79

L
Lambert, Chris 281
Lamborghini
  Countach 250
  Miura 21, 224
Lamborghini, Ferruccio 21
Lampredi, Aurelio 46, 52, 55,
  61, 68, 85, 87, 115, 162, **278**
Lancia 14
  D24 85
  D50 14
Lardi, Lina 14
Lardi, Piero 14, 22, 27

Lauda, Niki 23, 278, **281**
Le Mans 24 Hours 11, 17, 20,
  142, 169, 194, 204
Leopold III, of Belgium 46,
  51, 213
Levegh, Pierre 142
Lunn, Roy 20
Lurani, Count Giovanni
  'Johnny' 187

M
McAfee, Ernie 85
Macklin, Lance 142
McLaren 25
  F1 259, 267
McQueen, Steve 194
Maglioli, Umberto 68
Magnum, P.I. 254
Martin, Paolo 233, 247, 249
Martinengo, Franco 90
Marzotto, Count Umberto 39
Marzotto, Vittorio 85
Maserati 11, 15, 22
  MC12 270
Massimino, Alberto 12
Meregalli, Guido 9
Michelotti, Giovanni 15, 39,
  278–79

Mille Miglia 12, 13, 31, 52, 85
Montezemolo, Luca di 23,
  26
Moss, Stirling 142, 155
Mubadala Development
  Comapny 27
Murray, James 106, 108
Musso, Luigi 142

N
Nazi Party, German 11
Nuvolari, Tazio 11

P
Pike, Roy 194
Pinin Farina/Pininfarina 16,
  46, 52, 61, 68, 85, 90, 106,
  115, 133, 149, 155, 162, 166,
  169, 194, 237
Pininfarina, Sergio 22
Pirelli, Leopoldo 213
Portago, Alfonso Antonio
  Vicente Eduardo
  Angel Blas Francisco
  de Borja Cabeza de
  Vaca y Leighton,
  17th Marquis de 133
Prost, Alain 25

R

Regazzoni, Gianclaudio 'Clay' 23, **281**
Rethy, Princess Lilian de 213
Ricart, Wilfredo 12
Road & Track 18, 173, 247
Rocchi, Franco 204, 254, 262
Rossellini, Roberto 16, 74
Rubirosa, Porfirio 85, 89, 138
Rudd, Bill 173

S

Sage, Jean 127
Savona, Mario 74
Scaglietti 74, 79, 85, 127, 133, 149, 155, 159, 178, 187, 194, 218, 224
Scaglietti, Sergio 74, 142, **279**
    see also Scaglietti
Scheckter, Jody 24, 278
Schumacher, Michael 26–27, **281**
Sebring 12 Hours 127, 142, 240
Shelby, Carroll 20
Sivocci, Ugo 8, 9
Sommer, Raymond 31
Stewart, Jackie 233
Surtees, John 19, 20, **282**
Swaters, Jacques 7–8

T

Tadini, Mario 11
Taramazzo, Luigi 120
Targa Florio 8–9, 13, 142
Tavoni, Romolo 17
Tjaarda, Tom 213, **279**

Todt, Jean 26
Tomaso, Alejandro de 99
Tour de France 61, 133
Tourist Trophy 79, 155
Trintignant, Maurice 79
Trips, Wolfgang 'Taffy' von 17

V

Victor Emmanuel III 10
Vignale, Alfredo 15, 16, 39, 46, 52, 61, 68, 72, 278
Villeneuve, Gilles 24, **282**
Villoresi, Luigi 'Gigi' 68, 85
Volpi di Misurata, Count Giovanni 138
von Neumann, John 127, 149

W

Walker, Rob 155
Weber carburettors 52, 76, 113, 155, 204
White, Kirk 240
Wilke, Bob 99, 104
Wilkins, Gordon 39
Williams 25
World Drivers' Championships 7, 13, 14, 17, 18, 23, 27
World Sportscar Championships 127, 142, 178
Wyer, John 20

Z

Zagato 120, 125, 133, 213, 262